A Straight T

Psycnological Treatments for Mental Health Problems

David Pilgrim

PCCS BOOKS
Ross-on-Wye

First published in 2009

PCCS BOOKS Ltd
2 Cropper Row
Alton Road
Ross-on-Wye
Herefordshire
HR9 5LA
UK
Tel +44 (0)1989 763900
www.pccs-books.co.uk

**A Straight Talking Introduction to
Psychological Treatments for Mental Health Problems**

A CIP catalogue record for this book is available from the British Library

ISBN 978 1 906254 16 2

Cover designed in the UK by Old Dog Graphics
Typeset in the UK by The Old Dog's Missus
Printed in the UK by Ashford Colour Press, Gosport, Hampshire

Contents

* Because there are so many types of psychological treatment discussed, David Pilgrim has included a comprehensive Glossary (pp. 101–20). You will find these terms in SMALL CAPITALS throughout the text.

Introduction to the *Straight Talking* series

What are mental health problems?

Much of what is written and spoken about emotional distress or mental health problems implies that they are illnesses. This can lead us all too easily to believe that we no longer have to think about mental health problems, because illness is best left to doctors. They are the illness experts, and psychiatrists are the doctors who specialise in mental illness. This series of books is different because we don't think that all mental health problems should be automatically regarded as illnesses.

If mental health problems aren't necessarily illnesses, it means that the burden of responsibility for distress in our lives should not be entirely shouldered by doctors and psychiatrists. All citizens have a responsibility, however small, in creating a world where everyone has a decent opportunity to live a fulfilling life. This is a contentious idea, but one which we want to advance alongside the dominant medical view.

Rather than accept that solutions to mental health problems are 'owned' by the medical profession, we will take a good look at alternatives which involve the users of psychiatric services, their carers, families, friends and other 'ordinary people' taking control of their own lives. One of the tools required in order to become active in mental health issues, whether your own or other people's, is knowledge. This series of books is a starting point for anyone who wants to know more about mental health.

How these books are written

We want these books to be understandable, so we use everyday language wherever possible. The books could have been almost completely jargon-free, but we thought that including some technical and medical terms would be helpful. Most doctors, psychiatrists and psychologists use the medical model of mental illness and manuals to help them diagnose mental health problems. The medical model and the diagnostic manuals use a particular set of terms to describe what doctors think of as 'conditions'. Although these words aren't very good at describing individual people's experiences, they are used a lot in psychiatric and psychological services, so we thought it would be helpful to define these terms as we went along and use them in a way that might help readers understand what the professionals mean. We don't expect that psychiatrists and psychologists and others working in mental health services will stop using medical terminology (although we think it might be respectful for them to drop it when talking to their patients and their families), so these books should help you get used to, and learn *their* language.

The books also contain resources for further learning (pp. 120–3). As well as lists of books, websites and organisations at the end of the book, there are endnotes. These will not be important to everyone, but they do tell the reader where information – a claim about effectiveness, an argument for or against, or a quotation – has come from so you can follow it up if you wish.

Being realistic and reassuring

Our aim is to be realistic – neither overly optimistic nor pessimistic. Things are nearly always more complicated than we would like them to be. Honest evaluations of mental health problems, of what might cause them, of what can help, and of what the likely outcome might be, are, like so much in life, somewhere in between. For the vast majority of people it would be wrong to say that they have an illness from which they will never recover. But it would be equally wrong to say that they will be completely unchanged by the distressing thoughts and feelings they are having. Life is an accumulation of experiences. There is usually no pill, or any other treatment for that matter, that will take us back to 'how we were before'. There are many things we can do (and we will be looking at lots of them in this series) in collaboration with doctors, psychiatrists, psychologists, counsellors, indeed everyone working in mental health services, with the help of our friends and family, or on our own, which stand a good chance of helping us feel better and build a constructive life with hope for the future.

Of course, we understand that the experiences dealt with in these books can sometimes be so overwhelming, confusing and terrifying that people will try to escape from them by withdrawing, going mad or even by trying to kill themselves. This happens when our usual coping strategies fail us. We accept that killing oneself is, in some circumstances, a rational act – that for the person in question it can make a lot of sense. Nonetheless, we believe that much of the distress that underpins such an extreme course of action, from which there can be no turning back, is avoidable. For this reason, all of the books in this series point towards realistic hope and recovery.

Debates

There is no single convenient answer to many of the most important questions explored in these books. No matter how badly we might wish for a simple answer, what we have is a series of debates, or arguments more like, between stakeholders and there are many stakeholders whose voices demand space in these books. We use the word 'stakeholders' here because service users, carers, friends, family, doctors, psychologists, psychiatrists, nurses and other workers, scientists in drug companies, therapists, indeed all citizens, have a stake in how our society understands and deals with problems of mental health. It is simultaneously big business and intimately personal, and many things in between. As we go along, we try to explain how someone's stake in distress (including our own, where we can see it), whether business or personal, can influence their experience and judgement.

Whilst we want to present competing (sometimes opposing) viewpoints, we don't want to leave the reader high and dry to evaluate complicated debates on their own. We will try to present reasonable conclusions which might point in certain directions for personal action. Above all, though, we believe that knowledge is power and that the better informed you are, even though the information might be conflicting, the more able you will be to make sound decisions.

It's also useful to be reminded that the professionals involved in helping distressed people are themselves caught in the same flow of conflicting information. It is their *job*, however, to interpret it in our service, so that the best solutions are available to as many people as possible. You may have noticed that the word 'best' brings with it certain challenges, not least of all, what we mean when we use this term. Perhaps the best means the most effective? However, even using words like 'effective' doesn't completely clear up the puzzle. An effective treatment could be the one which returns someone to work quickly, if you are an employer, or one which makes someone feel happier and more calm, if they are your son or daughter. Readers will also know from recent press coverage that the National Institute for Health and Clinical Excellence (NICE) which evaluates and recommends treatments, keeps one eye on the budget, so 'effective' might mean 'cost effective' to some people. This brings us to evidence.

Evidence

Throughout these books there will be material which we will present as 'evidence'. This is one of the most contentious terms to be found in this series. One person's evidence is another person's fanciful mythology and yet another person's oppressive propaganda. Nevertheless the term crops up increasingly in everyday settings, most relevantly when we hear of 'evidence-based practice'. The idea behind this term is that the treatments psychologists and psychiatrists offer should be those that work. Crudely put, there should be some evidence that, say, talking about problems, or taking a prescribed drug, actually helps people to feel better. We encounter a real problem however, when trying to evaluate this evidence, as the books will demonstrate. We will try not to discount any 'evidence' out of hand, but we will evaluate it, and we will do this with a bias towards scientific evaluation.

The types of evidence that will be covered in these books, along with their positive and negative points, include the following.

Research methods, numbers and statistics

On the one hand, the logic of most research is simple, but on the other hand, the way things have to be arranged to avoid bias in the results can lead to a perplexing system of measurements. Even the experts lose the sense of it sometimes. We'll try to explain the logic of studies, but almost certainly leave out the details. You can look these up yourself if you wish.

The books in this series look at research into a wide range of issues regarding mental health problems, including the experience of distress, what is known about the causes of problems, and their prevention and treatment. Different research methods are more or less appropriate for each of these areas, so we will be looking at different types of research as we go along. We say this now because many readers may be most familiar with studies into the *effective treatments* of distress, and we want to emphasise that there are many credible and valid sources of essential information about distress that are sometimes overlooked.

You may have come across the idea that some research methods are 'better' than others – that they constitute a 'gold standard'. In the case of research into the effectiveness of different treatments, the gold standard is usually considered to be 'randomised controlled trials' (RCTs). In simple terms, RCTs are complex (and often very expensive) experiments in which a group of individuals who all suffer from the same problem are randomly allocated to a treatment or a 'control' condition (at its simplest, no treatment at all) to see whether the treatment works. We are not necessarily convinced that RCTs always *are* the best way of conducting research into effective treatments, but they are, at the present time, the method given most credence by bodies which control funding, such as the National Health Service's National Institute of Health and Clinical Excellence (NICE), so we need to understand them.

Personal experience

Personal experience is an important source of evidence to the extent that nowadays, people who have suffered debilitating psychiatric distress are sometimes called 'experts by experience'.

Personal stories provide an essential counterbalance to the impersonal numbers and statistics often found in research projects such as RCTs. Whilst not everyone is average, by definition, most people are. Balancing the average results obtained from RCTs with some personal stories helps complete the picture and is now widely accepted to the extent that it has given birth to the new field of 'survivor research'.

Understanding contexts

Widening our view to include the families and lives of people, and the cultural, economic, social and political settings in which we live completes the picture. Mental health problems are connected to the conditions in which we all live, just as much as they are connected to our biology. From the start we want readers to know that, if there is one message or model which the books are trying to get across, it is that problems in mental health are more often than not the result of complex events in the environments in which we live and our reactions to them. These reactions can also be influenced by our biology or the way we have learned to think and feel. Hopefully these books will help disentangle the puzzle of distress and provide positive suggestions and hope for us all, whether we work in the system, currently have mental health problems ourselves, are caring for someone or are friends with someone who has.

We hope that readers of these books will feel empowered by what they learn, and thereby more able to get the best out of mental health services. It would be wonderful if our efforts, directly or indirectly, influence the development of services that effectively address the emotional, social and practical needs of people with mental health problems.

Richard Bentall
Pete Sanders
April 2009

Chapter 1
Treating what?

People go to therapists for good reasons. They are in pain, they are unhappy, they feel some lack in their lives.[1]
Jeffrey Masson

Introduction

In this first chapter I explore the ways in which our understanding of mental abnormality relates to those offering psychological treatment and to those receiving psychological treatment. I think of psychological treatment as a set of professionally organised responses to psychological difference in society, whether these are identified by the 'patients' or 'clients' themselves, or by others. The term is shorthand for a range of interventions, which are called 'talking treatment', 'psychological therapy', 'counselling' or 'psychotherapy'.

My emphasis from the outset then is that therapy is a professional matter – people may seek solace and help for their problems, with or without success, from friends and family but they are not *in therapy*. This point is important because the person who is distressed or dysfunctional in their relationships only becomes a 'patient' or 'client' when opting into that role or when it is imposed upon them. However, it is also commonplace now for people to use the term 'therapeutic' to indicate that something in their lives is being experienced as being helpful. The language of therapy has insinuated its way into the public imagination.

I will slip between the labels of 'patient' and 'client' because no stable distinction can be made between them. I am aware though that some in the therapy industry mark out counselling positively as a set of practices without medical connotations or, negatively, as a shortened or superficial version of 'proper' therapy. I do not find these distinctions persuasive. The use of the words 'treatment' or 'therapy' brings with it medical connotations. Objecting to these, the psychiatrist and psychoanalyst Thomas Szsaz, has argued that because the mind can only be sick in a metaphorical sense, then mental illness is a myth and therefore it cannot be 'treated' or be the subject of 'therapy'. As a consequence, he argues, psychotherapy, like mental illness itself, is a 'myth'.[2] However, Szasz believes that a professional relationship involving talk can help people with their 'problems of living'. He offers instead the notion of 'iatrology' – a word that is harder to say and has not apparently been adopted even by those understanding the argument.

Maybe the positive option of using the term 'counselling' avoids the medicalising connotations. However, for now, those on the giving and receiving ends of the relationship still tend to use medicalised notions of 'therapy' and 'treatment', even though they might harbour doubts or criticisms about psychiatric diagnosis. This first chapter sets out some arguments about this ambivalence from psychological therapists and their clients. If people seek or are prescribed psychological treatment what is being treated? The question can be put slightly differently – what is the subjective experience of mental health problems and what is the social context of that experience?

Below I explore the use of psychological treatments in relation to misery (which is largely self-labelled); madness (largely labelled by others); and troubled and troublesome individuals (those who are habitually unhappy and/or they recurrently distress others). In practice, all three may be jumbled up – mental health problems come in all shapes and sizes and emerge in a variety of contexts. Also, an individual patient may move over time between different forms of deviance or dysfunction and this shift may elicit changes in diagnosis when they are in contact with mental health services. It is not unusual to find in the case notes of those in prolonged contact with services that their diagnosis keeps changing. We can expect that 'symptom profiles' or 'presenting problems' will overlap and flux over time.

However, by presenting these three groups in this way, I am seeking deliberately to reframe and discuss what in psychiatric terms are broadly called 'the neuroses', 'the psychoses', and 'the personality disorders', as varieties of personal and social judgements. As Mary Boyle[3] points out in her critique of psychiatric diagnosis, it starts and ends with labels rather than engaging with and truly exploring the *content* of the symptoms they comprise. For example, if 'schizophrenia' is a formal medical label for what lay people have already noted (that the identified patient is speaking to voices others do not hear and believes that people are conspiring against them) what advantage is the diagnosis and to whom? Or in another instance, where a patient is very miserable and has lost interest in food and sex and takes themselves to their GP to be diagnosed with 'depression', what has been achieved?

Basically, a diagnosis is a very crude starting point. It begs many questions about distress and dysfunction. Where do the symptoms of mental disorder come from? What do they mean? What value or lack of value might we place on them? Is distress and oddity part of the human condition or a sign of pathology? Should we medicalise psychological problems, turning people into patients, or view them in a different way? These (and other) questions can only be answered if we address the nuances of mental health problems as personally expressed experiences in particular social contexts. Diagnosis in itself offers us nothing in this regard.

Going round in circles: Professional and lay terminology

'Misery' and 'madness' are found in common speech. Ordinary language is used to describe distress and inexplicable deviance. What professional classification systems like the *Diagnostic and Statistical Manual of Mental Disorders* (DSM-IV) published by the American Psychiatric Association[4] and *International Statistical Classification of Diseases and Related Health Problems 10th Revision* (ICD-10) published by the World Health Organization[5] provide is a gloss on these words. For example, 'schizophrenia' replaces 'madness' when doctors rubber-stamp lay decisions.[6] Thus, 'mental health problems' or 'psychological distress' are not mere medical artefacts (even Szasz does not deny the personal reality of people experiencing 'problems of living'). These personal troubles and experiences of distress and dysfunction are not invented by mental health professionals – the latter codify problems but they do not invent them from thin air. Put differently, for clarity, diagnoses are medical inventions but misery and madness exist with or without them.

In my view, technical terms like 'mental illness' or 'mental disorder', especially specific diagnoses like 'schizophrenia' or 'depression', tell us nothing new – there is, as they say, 'no added value'. Why not just say that people are 'mad' or 'crazy', or 'miserable' or 'sad' or 'anxious' or 'frightened'? Even moralistic terms such as 'cowardly' or 'evil' may be less mystifying than diagnoses of say 'avoidant personality disorder' or 'dissocial personality disorder'.

Rather than turning ordinary attributions about suffering and oddity into medical labels, professionals could become adept at exploring why people have these distressed and sometimes distressing experiences and how we might successfully reduce or reverse them. This represents the true practical challenge for therapists. The common medical obsession with getting the diagnosis 'right', when psychiatrists try to express and maintain their precarious professional authority over psychological abnormality, is at best a trivial starting point. At worst it is a stigmatising diversion from dealing with personal and social complexity. To be clear though, I am not of the view that diagnosis is merely or only a display of medical power, as other interests are at work – a point I return to below.

If we look at the way in which legal decisions are made about the presence or absence of mental illness, this conclusion about the relevance of ordinary descriptions or 'lay attributions' is confirmed. For example, in 1974 Judge Lawton said that the term 'mental illness' reflected 'ordinary words of the English language. They have no particular medical significance. They have no particular legal significance.' Lawton refers back to the opinion of another Law Lord, Lord Reid, who suggested that when he was present and a defendant's mental state was at issue:

> I ask myself what would the ordinary sensible person have said about the patient's condition in this case if he had been informed of his behaviour? In my judgement such a person would have said 'Well the fellow is obviously mentally ill'.[7]

As a result of this ruling, we now have what is called the 'man-must-be-mad' test.[8] We are sane by common consent and we get to say who is outside of the group. Medical expertise is not generally required. Most of us most of the time are aware if others act or speak in an unintelligible way. Most know what it is like to feel sad or frightened. These are ordinary human observations about inner feelings and outer norms.

The many legal, scientific, logical and sociological criticisms that have been made and remade about psychiatric diagnosis over the past hundred years have not led to its demise.[9]

Moreover, many psychiatrists have been some of the strongest critics of diagnosis and many non-psychiatrists (including psychologists and psychotherapists) have held on to it. Other groups such as the drug companies and some though not all patients and relatives also embrace diagnosis at times.

Lobby groups dominated by relatives of people with a diagnosis of depression accept its scientific status as a brain disease without question.[10] But many in the mental health service users' movement consider that diagnosis is just an unhelpful part of a stigmatising social process. And there is further variability. Some patient lobby groups celebrate their diagnosis and campaign for its greater recognition. A good example in this regard is those with or seeking the exotic 'multiple personality disorder' or 'dissociative identity disorder'.[11] By contrast few patients chase the damning label of 'schizophrenia'. In other words, diagnosis may be celebrated by some patients and resented and rejected by others and some diagnoses seem to be more helpful or offensive than others to their recipients.

Recently in Britain the government offered the following new definition of mental disorder:

'Mental disorder' means an impairment of or disturbance in the functioning of the mind or brain resulting from any disability or disorder of the mind or brain.[12]

This is a tautological, and so not very persuasive, definition.[13] The whole is explained by the part and vice versa. Q: How do you know that the person has a disorder of the mind or brain? A: Because they are acting or speaking in an impaired or dysfunctional way. Q: Why do they act in this odd way? A: Because they are mentally disordered.

This is a variation on the tautological way in which all FUNCTIONAL MENTAL DISORDERS have been defined for the past century. Q: How do we know this patient is schizophrenic? A: Because they hear voices and they express strange and rigid

6

beliefs. Q: Why do they report these odd experiences? A: Because they suffer from schizophrenia. And so it goes on. Moreover, the new definition by the Department of Health adds a further confusion by talking of the brain – does this mean that all neurology patients are mentally disordered?

To restate an earlier point, although these dubious technical attempts to define mental illness or mental disorder are not persuasive, this does not mean that people do not have problems. Remember that even Szasz when rejecting psychiatric diagnosis does not deny that people have 'problems of living'. My argument here is simply that we might develop a greater understanding if we understand why people have these problems in the social and biographical context of their particular lives, past and present.

This line of reasoning is not new. It is derived from the work of the Swiss psychiatrist Adolf Meyer and was reinforced subsequently by that group of psychiatrists in the 1960s, dubbed 'anti-psychiatrists' and then after the 1980s called 'critical psychiatrists'. However, it is weakly developed in modern psychiatry compared to the dominant model offered at the turn of the twentieth century by Emil Kraepelin.[14] Kraepelin asserted that mental disorders are naturally occurring states, which reflect inherited damage to the nervous system. This assertion emphasises genetic determination and the role of brain diseases in explaining abnormal experience and behaviour.

Having looked at the difficulty legislators have had to create abstract catch-all definitions of mental disorder or mental illness, in practice decisions are idiosyncratic and context-specific. Professionals actually place a gloss on what ordinary people have already decided – they 'codify' lay judgements. As the discussion above indicated this codification generally coincides with the general intention of the non-professional. For example, despite psychiatric professionals trying to special plead that police officers are unable to accurately identify mental disorder the latter tend to

7

'deem' someone to be mentally disordered in a way that is later confirmed by specialists.

However, this general pattern of concurrence, which tends to point to a 'rubber-stamping' role for mental health workers, is uneven. Occasionally professionals will seek to normalise or reassure when lay people want a clear label of abnormality. For example, at times parents may be keen to have their children diagnosed with Asperger's syndrome or Attention Deficit Hyperactive Disorder (ADHD), whereas their treating professionals may not agree readily to the diagnostic task. Also, in the other direction, some lay judgements want to deny the presence of mental disorder. Moreover, professionals themselves may disagree about its presence.

Implications of diagnosis for the notion of 'treatment'

The above discussion suggests that the word 'treatment' for our purposes is complicated. In its narrow sense, of treating a diagnosed medical condition, then it can be used, but with caution, because it is a matter of debate whether psychological difference in society is validly codified by medical labels. But if it is used in this medical sense, then the normal rules of assessing the effectiveness of a medical treatment can, or even should, be applied. These rules involve the use of randomised controlled trials (RTCs) (see Chapter 4 for more on these) to check whether a treatment works.

If we use a broader notion of 'treatment', with its moral connotation, then more questions can be posed. For example, are people with mental health problems tolerated and respected by others? Does society incorporate their talents or are they socially excluded? Do people with mental health problems have the same human rights as other citizens? Does treating them medically help or hinder in the latter regard?

Consensual and imposed psychological treatment

Until the end of the nineteenth century, treatment, in both its narrow and wide senses, was largely about dealing with lunacy. Indeed, even today, the major controversies about social exclusion and human rights centre on madness or 'severe and enduring mental illness', which includes those with diagnoses of 'schizophrenia' and 'bipolar disorder'. But in the past 100 years, the responsibility of psychiatry and related professions has broadened substantially on two fronts beyond madness.

On the first, neurotic misery has become the concern of a whole range of mental health experts offering forms of talking treatment, and the medicinal treatment approach to 'common mental disorders' has largely shifted to general practitioners and other primary mental health care workers. Neurotic misery (people outside of asylums recognising that they were distressed and wanting help) was labelled before the turn of the twentieth century but it was not of great interest or concern to medicine. That picture changed radically after the First World War when asylum psychiatry was augmented by outpatient psychotherapy for dysfunctional community-based patients. This shift emerged because of the psychological casualties returning from the war with the label of 'shellshock'.

On the second front, the management of the risk to self and others from a range of problem behaviours has been incorporated into mental health work. These problem behaviours include patients abusing substances and those with recurring interpersonal difficulties – what are typically now called 'the personality disorders'. The inclusion of these psychosocial problems into mental health work reduced the range of traditional ethical and legal responses to fecklessness, cowardice, immaturity, intoxication, selfishness and amorality into a single medical response of diagnosis and treatment. It was only after the First World War that these psychosocial problems were turned into medical-psychiatric problems. Soon intoxication and personality problems were to become forms of mental disorder and psychiatry was to take control and authority over them.

Therapeutic bureaucracies now exist, such as the NHS in Britain. These contain services in which the fee is not evident. Moreover, parts of these therapeutic bureaucracies contain those who are in receipt of therapy but are not voluntarily in the patient role. Can the term 'psychological treatment' be used validly if the recipient resists and resents the imposed patient role, say in an acute psychiatric unit? A start to answering this question involves accepting that there is a continuum that exists between voluntary and involuntary patient–professional contact (see Figure 1).

Figure 1: *The Continuum of Voluntarism*

Non-intervention	Voluntary treatment	Pseudo-voluntary treatment	Involuntary treatment	Treatment in secure setting

This continuum provides a context for understanding treatment. Because it is a continuum, individual recipients of treatment may move to and fro along it in the patient role. Also professionals may work in different contexts, where points on the continuum predominate. For example, the implications of providing a particular form of treatment are different in an outpatient setting than in an acute unit or a secure hospital. And, with the exception of 'treatment in conditions of security', the extent of coercion does not neatly correlate with the physical setting. For example, a patient can voluntarily admit themselves for treatment to an inpatient setting. By contrast, in some mental health systems outpatients may be treated involuntarily. To highlight the ways in which the points on the continuum shade into one another, I will briefly examine adjacent pairings.

Non-intervention / voluntary treatment

Examples at this interface are brief and intermittent therapies which focus on a light touch and allow the patient to spend the great bulk of their time solving their own problems on a daily basis. Some types of talking therapy, such as SOLUTION-FOCUSED BRIEF THERAPY and Short-Term Dynamic Therapy[15] have this light touch emphasis. RE-FRAMING and NORMALISATION are also techniques, which try to look at the patient's problems in a different way and enable them to be experienced as less problematic. Some authors have noted that much of the emphasis in the talking treatments is to enable the patient to realise that the solutions exist within themselves. This logical outcome implies the need to give up dependency on the therapist as quickly as possible. However, a criticism of mental health interventions has been that the opposite scenario is more common – that patients may become chronically reliant on treatments offered to them.

Pseudo-voluntary and involuntary treatment

Pseudo-voluntarism refers to the gap between the formal status of a patient (they are recorded for administrative purposes as voluntarily agreeing to treatment offered) and background pressures, which invalidate true freedom of choice. For example, a drug user may be offered outpatient therapy as an alternative to imprisonment for possession of an illegal substance. In another example, a therapist may reserve the right to invoke coercive powers if the patient becomes suicidal. Thus there are contingencies which lead to professional power being exercised unilaterally to shift the status of the patient from being a true volunteer to one in which they are coerced into accepting treatment. The commonest example here is of psychiatric patients who are in outpatient therapy but are re-admitted involuntarily to hospital ('sectioned' in the UK) at times when service providers consider them a risk to themselves or others.

Whereas patients forcibly detained and treated in acute psychiatric facilities are being treated coercively, those in higher conditions of security are subject to far greater physical containment. High-security hospitals (in England, for example Broadmoor and Ashworth) are like high-security prisons. Also, the acute patient typically leaves hospital after a few weeks or months, whereas the mentally disordered offender is usually incarcerated for many years. However, the acute patient has committed no crime and they are detained without trial (or its equivalent of an advocate arguing for their freedom). Both the non-offender and the offender receive treatments that they may not want. Both may be secluded (put in solitary confinement) as inpatients.

In the next and final chapters I return to this question about where therapy takes place as one of the key defining features of psychological treatment.

Reflections on what is being treated

Given that psychiatric diagnoses are controversial and treatment exists on a continuum of coercion, what can we say with certainty about mental health problems and their management?

• Mental disorder is not *merely* the by-product of professional activity. No matter how critical one is of the logic and content of turning madness and misery into medical categories, we know that concerns about how to respond to behavioural difference preceded psychiatry. The tendency to label, separate, stereotype and stigmatise those whose actions are difficult to understand or who are too distressed to fulfil their roles as adult citizens appears to be a long-lived and universal pattern.

• Mental health problems are often defined or labelled by lay people *before* professional intervention. This lay labelling can be applied by third parties or by the incipient patient. In other words, emotional or psychological deviance is negotiated socially. This social negotiation suggests that those psychiatrists who argue that their diagnoses reflect naturally occurring forms of abnormality (emphasising genetic inheritance and brain disease), which exist universally over time, are simply wrong in their logic. I mentioned that this conventional wisdom in psychiatry was in line with the view of Emil Kraepelin. I consider that this Kraepelinian tradition is a crude and unhelpful response to the complexities of people's problems.

• So-called 'common mental health problems' of fear and depression seem to fit this universal and trans-historical assumption, by and large. For example, the physiological markers of anxiety (such as sweating, palpitations, muscle tension and hypertension) are biologically predictable when all mammals (i.e. not just humans) are faced with frightening stimuli. However, what a person is anxious *about* reflects the social conditions they exist in and the meanings they attach to those conditions. As for depression, it is true that mammals can be reduced to misery by constant stress and loss – they develop learned helplessness. But there are some cultures that have no word for depression. How then can we claim, as many now do, that depression is a universal pandemic? And how people see their situation affects how miserable they are. Thus we have to understand *meanings* not just causes when studying mental health problems in humans.

• Madness is essentially about the failure of some people to render their rule-breaking behaviour intelligible to others when requested. Whether this failure reflects choice or incompetence is not really relevant. It is the *fact* that some people act in an unintelligible and unaccountable way in the eyes of those around them (who are sane by common consent) which leads to a label of insanity. Diagnosing the latter as 'schizophrenia' or 'bipolar disorder' is a medical gloss on a lay judgement. However, being out of step or unintelligible (hallmarks of madness) have not always been pathologised or evaluated negatively. For example, Socrates, Pythagoras, the Prophet Mohammed, Joan of Arc and Luther all hallucinated. Jesus Christ and the Buddha both made certain and grandiose claims about the meaning of life that neither could substantiate. These figures now have hyper-credibility rather than the invalidation awaiting most patients with a diagnosis of schizophrenia.

• When we turn to troubled and troublesome individuals more ambiguity arises. Whereas madness has been considered and responded to since antiquity and neurosis has become a common and sympathetic concern of us all in Western societies (Freud noted that neurosis is the norm), mental health professionals remain ambivalent in the face of chronic personality problems, fecklessness and intoxication. It is true that some professionals develop a niche expertise about this third group of 'mental disorders' but many avoid their treatment. Sometimes the label of 'personality disorder' is a reason for *not* offering treatment – a rationale for excluding patients from statutory mental health services. Thus there is a paradox about the notion of 'personality disorder' (PD). On the one hand it is deemed to occur in about ten per cent of the population. On the other hand there is a reluctance on the part of many mental health professionals (whatever their stance on the legitimacy of the diagnosis) to deal with this set of relatively common psychosocial problems in their midst. The particular challenge for psychological therapists is that medication, electroconvulsive therapy and psychosurgery have failed most in response to these difficulties. Not surprisingly then, even in biologically orientated and medically dominated acute psychiatric services it is often the case that psychological therapists are entreated to deal with these patients. The heart-sink effect of 'PD', 'complex cases' or 'dual diagnosis' is common in those services and therapists are often given the role of the cavalry coming over the hill to the rescue.

Chapter 2
What is psychological treatment?

> The irreducible elements of psychotherapy are a therapist, a
> patient, and a regular and reliable time and place.[1]
> *RD Laing*

> Counselling and psychotherapy have developed organically
> and, some critics would say, have flowed almost
> promiscuously into many areas of our lives, so that exactly
> what they are *for*, what their goals are, is not always clear.[2]
> *Colin Feltham*

Introduction

This chapter extends the discussion of the target of therapy to its
objectives and nature. Scanning a few text-based and web-based
definitions of psychological treatment (the reader can
immediately go on the web and have a look) three main
components are repeated. First, psychological treatment involves
a *personal relationship* between the therapist and their client.
Second, generally *talk* is the main vehicle involved in the
relationship and is the basis for the next component. Third, there
is an expectation that the relationship exists to *improve the mental
health of the client* – usually by negotiating or encouraging
changes in the way the person thinks, feels and acts.

With regard to the third component, psychological
treatment is distinguished from other forms of personal
intimacy – the relationship is there for the betterment of the
client not the therapist. Consequently, normal rules of intimacy

do not apply, so new ones need to be invented. In other forms of personal encounter, mental health gain may be affected positively (or negatively) but it is only in therapy that mental health gain is the prime *objective* of the relationship.

These three components create variations on a theme and inconsistencies. For example, the relationship may be with more than one client, yet the one-to-one notion of therapy dominates both lay and professional images of psychological treatment. I return to this point below and in Chapter 4. Despite the tendency to define therapy by one-to-one meetings, it can entail stranger groups (group therapy) or natural groups (family therapy). Also, although talk is the main vehicle for change, some varieties of therapy include artwork, music, drama and even bodywork or massage. The general taboo on personal touching in most psychological treatment is breached by the some of these deviations from the notion of 'talking treatment'.

With regard to the third defining feature of negotiating change, that the relationship exists to improve the mental health of the client, probably the best-known basis for modern therapy, PSYCHOANALYSIS, began primarily as a method to understand the unconscious. Indeed, even now, psychoanalysis proper (rather than PSYCHODYNAMIC THERAPY) has this main objective. Striving for personal change is not the main point of the analytical encounter. Thus even one of the core components, that of personal change, is open to question (though the importance of post-interpretive insight in psychoanalysis might indicate that it is implicitly seeking a form of change).

With these generalities and exceptions in mind, how does psychological treatment compare to other encounters in health settings between providers and users? The first point about the relationship is not exceptional. The great majority of all types of therapeutic interventions entail a practitioner–client relationship. It is true that some are fleeting and they hardly warrant the term 'relationship' (say, an hour in the dentist's chair, unable to speak because your mouth is full, once a year). Surgeons and anaesthetists spend the bulk of their time with a patient who does not talk back because they are in a deep sleep. But even in these cases of dental and general surgery, the patient has a personal experience of those treating them before and after the operation.

If we turn to health professions with 'therapy' in their title (physiotherapists, occupational therapists, speech therapists), the role of the relationship starts to become more extensive. Thus, the first defining feature in psychological treatment, the relationship, is noteworthy not because it is unique but because it is more at the centre of change. In other words other types of therapists develop a respectful collaboration in order to deploy interventions – a sort of means to an end. This is also the case in psychological treatment but more so – the relationship *is by and large* the intervention.

However, this stereotype of the relationship as always being the core, defining feature of psychological treatments can be challenged. For example, therapy can now be accessed impersonally by using computers, suggesting that even the personal relationship is potentially disposable in psychological treatment. The role of the relationship as a vehicle for change is still noteworthy though. When we return to the question of effectiveness in the final chapter, this point comes through strongly.

So, if the relationship is crucial but not unique to psychological treatment (with computers now even challenging this axiom) what about talk? The conversational emphasis in the great majority of psychological therapies is not in dispute. Indeed 'talking treatment' is one synonym for psychological treatment. Even in computer therapy a dialogue of sorts occurs. In other words, therapy is interactive; change, or a new reality or way of seeing the world, comes from some form of stylised or constructed dialogue. This can be contrasted with other forms of treatment, like surgery and medication, where compliance from, not conversation with, the patient is the main expectation.

The vocabulary of the talking therapies has largely shifted from 'patients' to 'clients', which probably reflects this greater emphasis on dialogue alongside expectations that clients will be increasingly responsible for their own behaviour. 'Patient' conveys the image of a person 'patiently' waiting, in a passive state, for the treatment applied to them to work. Even though psychoanalysis traditionally seeks to understand rather than change people, it clings on to the concept of the 'patient'. This contradiction is rooted in an historical paradox. Freud used interpretation on the one hand to study the unconscious and validate his emerging theory and, on the other hand, out of financial necessity he had to provide his version of medical treatment to neurotic patients. (He considered psychotic patients untreatable because they could not develop a TRANSFERENCE to the therapist.)

So is talk the defining feature of psychological treatment? Again, as with the relationship, it is central but not unique. Moreover, the way that words are used in psychological treatment varies from one type to another. For some the emphasis is on words as insights or hypotheses to be fed back to the client for the latter to take or leave. For others, they are used to communicate warmth, honesty and empathy as necessary and sufficient conditions for change.[3] For yet others, words are used to challenge the client's current way of acting, thinking and feeling.

More will be said about such differences later but what they already indicate is that if words are by their very fact at the centre of '*talking* treatments', they only indicate a loose relationship. Words and psychological treatments are like bricks and buildings. Talking treatments, like brick buildings, can end up looking remarkably different, even though they are constructed from a common material. If words are the bricks of therapy, then they can be used in a highly variable way to stylise the encounter. This variability is true of course across all human dialogues. For example, the type of conversation a mother has with her child is typically different in style and content from that held between a criminal and the police officer interrogating them. Talk is a resource for us all to use in a wide variety of ways.

The third component, acting only in the interest of the client and therefore involving an imbalance of power, is definitely not unique to the psychological treatments. As a consequence, the expectations of competence and integrity we have about any health practitioner also apply to therapy. However, one of the reasons that psychological treatments have been controversial is that they are so diverse that accurate and standardised judgements about competence are difficult to achieve. This is all the more so, as so much of therapy occurs in private, on a one-to-one basis. That problem has been compounded by the evidence about 'deterioration effects'. Deterioration effects refer to the client's mental health being aggravated, rather than improved, by therapy. I return to these points in the final chapter but now turn to the diversity that the 'bricks' of words create in the psychological treatments.

A theme I return to in this book is the common view that therapy is defined in its individual mode. For example, at the start of the chapter I began with Laing's definition of therapy: 'The irreducible elements of psychotherapy are a therapist, a patient, and a regular and reliable time and place.' But I would argue that diversity of setting and of types or models of therapy undermine such simple definitions. I now move to the challenge of diversity in the field, a field in which single models of therapy and ECLECTICISM are found side by side.

The challenge of treatment diversity

Imagine a client who has a few emotional difficulties in their life and a friend suggests that they seek therapy. This new experience can be informed by prior reading and recommendation or it may be a lottery. In the first instance, with enough money to pay, the client may target an approach broadly known to them. In the second case, their referral by their GP to a local therapist in the NHS will provide them with what is available. In both cases, even in the first where more knowledge is operating in advance of the first encounter, the client is largely in the dark and the therapist will control the interaction by the model of therapy they operate. This is even true when the model is client-centred or emphasises the collaborative effort to understand and improve the client's problems. The fact that the client is making the approach, vulnerable and relatively in the dark, and the therapist is well practised and understands the reasoning behind the type of therapy they offer creates an inevitable inequality of power and knowledge.

A good starting point for the reader about differences between common styles of therapy is Colin Feltham's book, *Which Psychotherapy? Leading exponents explain their differences.*[4] I also help to explain some of these differences in a little more detail in the Glossary at the end of the book (pp. 101–22).

In *Models of Influence in Psychotherapy,* Pentony[5] provides us with a way of understanding the range of therapies. He starts with a premise, which is even more pertinent now, that extensive theoretical and practical diversity characterise the field of interest to us. This diversity leads to the nigh impossibility of generating precise catch-all definitions of psychological treatment (hence my struggle above and my objection to Laing's simple boiled-down definition). This is frustrating for all concerned. What Pentony goes on to offer, and I summarise here, is a set of organising principles. These offer us a way of discussing psychological treatments, which accepts their diversity but also explains what they have in common.

Pentony's second main premise is that although unplanned encounters might bring about personal change, only the psychological treatments have *planned rationales,* or reasoned explanations, for the change process. Therapists from different therapeutic schools may disagree on *what* that rationale is but they all *have* a rationale. Indeed one of the common features of being trained in any therapy is that all initiates develop sufficient competence at *accounting* for their rationale in client contact to convince their supervisor that they are trustworthy in practice. Even today, many forms of supervision only entail listening to the account of trainees after the event – supervisors usually do not see them actually at work. In other words, the trainee develops a persuasive link between theory and practice. More experienced therapists become more confident in this regard with time.

Pentony is correct, for this reason, to emphasise that whilst personal change can occur in a whole range of encounters outside of therapy, what marks out therapy is the *production of rationales* by those trained in the therapy trade. Thus, if we are to understand psychological treatments, we have to understand how therapists understand human problems – what 'theory', 'model', 'paradigm' or even 'mythology' do they adhere to?

His third main point is that the diverse range of therapies can be grouped into three types of rationale for change: the placebo model, the resocialisation model, and the contextual model. Each of these will now be summarised.

- *The Placebo Model* of change in therapy is named after the well-known phenomenon that inert substances can lead to healing in general medicine. This is why double-blind trials of drugs often lead to the 'dummy wing' of the trial leading to clinical improvement. This might sound as though the 'placebo effect' is trivial or irrelevant but the reverse is true.

It is remarkable because it draws attention to the potential power of the therapist's personality *and* the expectations or faith in the therapist from the recipient of treatment. Just as confidence tricks are as much about the confidence of the duped party as the trickster, this two-way faith might also apply to therapy.

A number of mental health professionals emphasised this dimension to therapy[6] or even elevated it into an explicit rationale for organising therapy.[7] Torrey noted the healing strategies that witchdoctors and psychotherapists had in common.[8] Also, theologians have noted the parallels between Eastern ways and secular forms of therapy.[9] These authors discuss, for example, change in religious conversion and behaviour therapy and argue that the placebo model is about social influence.

The persuasiveness of the placebo model is rooted in three pertinent research-based findings. First, therapists from completely different schools can be effective (and vary in their effectiveness).

Second, some schools such as PERSON-CENTRED THERAPY and EXISTENTIAL THERAPY emphasise that the basis of change largely rests with the personal qualities of the therapist engaging with the client's unique experience and agency. For example, for Carl Rogers, the founder of person-centred therapy, the therapist's genuineness, warmth and empathy were the necessary and sufficient rationale for change. The critical point here is that these conditions were deemed to be *sufficient*, implying that technique and theory in therapy were of secondary importance. They might even be irrelevant. (I argue in Chapter 4 that paradoxically they are not irrelevant but only because they instil confidence in the relationship.) Indeed these conditions were demonstrated as important in early empirical studies of counselling.[10]

Third, studies of some technique-based therapies, such

as behaviour therapy, find that if components are altered or removed *the technique remains effective*.[11]

• *The Resocialisation Model* of therapeutic change is suggested by Schein,[12] who argues that many forms of therapy are about clients going through a learning cycle. First their current attitudes and habits are challenged (the 'demolition phase'). The first step in therapy is for the client to recognise that old habits must change – hence those who are content with their current lot will not be good therapy candidates. Once this need for change is established in principle, then therapists use forms of challenge to motivate the patient to reconstrue, or reinterpret their lives. This effect has both a cognitive and emotional dimension, with the client feeling anxious or even guilty about their personal status quo.

Second, as a result of the personal status quo for the client being destabilised, they are then open to change (the 'transitional stage'). Therapists at this juncture offer the clients new ways of talking about their lives. New options are rehearsed and new ways of judging what kind of life is desired are negotiated.

The third ('refreezing') phase involves settling on new ideas about the world and new habits and incorporating them routinely into their lives. (Freud called this 'working through', a term that therapists from a number of schools still use.) This may take some time because if a client changes then this will affect their relationships with others. Adjusted roles are thus anticipated for more than the client.

This model is about ditching old learned patterns of thought, feeling and relating to others and successfully experimenting with new ones. Strong resonances of this rationale can be found in BEHAVIOUR THERAPY, COGNITIVE BEHAVIOUR THERAPY, PERSONAL CONSTRUCT THERAPY,

PSYCHODYNAMIC THERAPY and RATIONAL EMOTIVE THERAPY. Although this list contains therapies seemingly at odds with one another (their advocates are certainly competitive and at times antagonistic), the three phases discussed by Schein can be identified in each.

• *The Contextual Model* has something in common with the placebo model in that it relies on social influence but is more complex in its formulation of change. It is mainly derived from therapists working with families.[13] The emphasis is more present–future oriented and less about insights about the past than in the resocialisation model. Much of it has been influenced by GENERAL SYSTEMS THEORY, which suggests that small changes can lead to large impacts.

At the start of the therapy neither the therapist nor the client know what these small changes to take and test out in the open system of their life might be. Contextual therapists are opportunistic in trying a range of suggestions or challenges in the particular context of the person's life and the way they interpret and apply them. In this sense they immediately experiment with the transitional and refreezing phases of the above model *at the same time* (no boundary between the two is explicitly recognised and the first phase of demolition is simply ignored or taken for granted). The therapist may be accused of being more manipulative than in the other two models. For example, it is common for people in distress to want to dwell on their problems but contextual therapists may deliberately ignore that expressed need and focus on a different type of conversation instead (e.g. SOLUTION-FOCUSED BRIEF THERAPY).

In another example, in STRUCTURAL FAMILY THERAPY, paradoxical instructions might be given (prescribing the symptom of the problem), such as suggesting that an insomniac might stay awake as long as possible. At the centre of all contextual approaches is the emphasis on narration (telling a different story and re-framing) rather than interpretation as practised by dynamic therapy, or the behavioural homework of behaviour therapy. In the postmodern version of the contextual model Lax emphasises that:

> Psychotherapy is the process of shifting the client's current 'problematic' discourse to another discourse that is more fluid and allows for a broader range of possible interactions.[14]

Having noted the three models suggested by Pentony I now want to draw out some of the implications of their similarities and differences.

Taking stock of the variety

The client's view of this diversity might be one of perplexity – indeed the more that we know of the large marketplace of therapy the more it buzzes in a state of apparent organised chaos. The three groupings of therapies suggested by Pentony above were one attempt to create order out of chaos. Literally hundreds of types of therapy exist, creating a minefield of understanding for those seeking help. They are not equally prevalent though. Moreover, the commoner forms of therapy in the marketplace of private therapy and in publicly funded health care systems can be grouped into 'extended families' or 'pedigrees'. If we look to edited handbooks of therapy we find that only a limited range of therapies are represented and within their lists there are 'family' connections.

For example, in Windy Dryden's *Handbook of Individual Therapy*[15] there are thirteen types of therapy listed. Three of these are derived explicitly from classical psychoanalysis and so are labelled 'psychodynamic therapy' (Freudian, Kleinian and

Jungian). For some reason Dryden puts Adlerian therapy separately, even though Jung parted company with Freud just as much as Adler (having both been originally part of Freud's trusted circle). Thus, four from thirteen on Dryden's list seem to be derived from Freud's original work, with individual clients in private practice.

Then three are listed by Dryden which share a common focus on biographical uniqueness (PERSON-CENTRED THERAPY, PERSONAL CONSTRUCT THERAPY and EXISTENTIAL THERAPY). These are connected through their philosophical roots in PHENOMENOLOGY and HUMANISM as is another listed, Berne's TRANSACTIONAL ANALYSIS (TA), with some aspects of EXISTENTIALISM and psychoanalysis also clearly influential. TA, like two others listed, COGNITIVE ANALYTICAL THERAPY (CAT) and GESTALT THERAPY reflect a hybrid or confluence of previous schools. In the case of CAT both psychoanalysis and personal-construct theory are evident. In the case of GESTALT, multiple influences are evident in its founder, Perls', writings (PSYCHOANALYSIS, GESTALT PSYCHOLOGY and Reichian Therapy). The latter, which is not listed separately by Dryden, was a radical variant of Freudianism that moved from talk to bodywork.

The remaining therapies (cognitive therapy, BEHAVIOUR THERAPY and RATIONAL EMOTIVE THERAPY) are sufficiently close in orientation that they are all represented in membership of the British Association for Behavioural and Cognitive Psychotherapy. They are all clear examples of Pentony's resocialisation model and all of them expect forms of behavioural homework be carried out between sessions.

I mentioned that the analysis of the listings in Dryden's book referred to individual therapy. The fact that the thirteen approaches to therapy listed contain no examples from Pentony's third paradigm (the contextual model) is telling. Whilst individual therapists will often be aware of the latter,

Dryden is correct to reflect its lack of practical impact by not including it in his list. This highlights that those from a family therapy tradition are a distinct culture that operates separately from those doing one-to-one therapy.

This sense of separation is not the case though in group therapy (where at times therapists work with individuals on a one-to-one basis, as well as within groups). In group therapy, Dryden's list of approaches are replicated but are biased more towards psychodynamic[16] and humanistic models.[17] The application of these models in a group rather than a one-to-one setting has created a different body of knowledge about processes (ways in which change comes about). Whereas the language of one-to-one therapy is about TRANSFERENCE, COUNTER-TRANSFERENCE and the WORKING ALLIANCE, in group work other processes are also described.

Potentially, group therapy provides elements of Pentony's placebo, resocialisation and contextual models. However, social influence is present beyond that of the therapist alone. For this reason, Pentony draws attention towards the proximity of group therapy to ideological reorientation or 'brainwashing'. Group members have the opportunity to share common experiences (reducing their isolation). They can imitate functional behaviour in other group members. They can experience a re-enactment of their own and others' families in the group setting. Multiple opportunities for interpersonal learning exist in groups and new forms of conduct can be tried out between group sessions.

The Sage Handbook of Counselling and Psychotherapy, edited by Colin Feltham and Ian Horton,[18] includes a chapter on contextual psychology and another on family therapy. However, these are overshadowed by the space allocated to the traditional models of individual work listed in Dryden noted above.

The editors offer a similar listing of main therapies to Dryden but cluster them slightly differently. Under a grouping of 'psychodynamic approaches' we find five (Adlerian, Freudian, Kleinian, Jungian and the ATTACHMENT THEORY of Bowlby). Under 'cognitive behavioural approaches' we find four (BEHAVIOURAL, COGNITIVE, PERSONAL CONSTRUCT, and RATIONAL EMOTIVE BEHAVIOUR THERAPY). More are elaborated than in Dryden under 'humanistic-existential approaches' (EXISTENTIAL, GESTALT, NARRATIVE, PERSON-CENTRED, PRIMAL, PSYCHODRAMA, PSYCHOSYNTHESIS and TRANSACTIONAL ANALYSIS). Six are listed under 'eclectic-integrative approaches' (COGNITIVE ANALYTICAL, MULTIMODAL, NEURO-LINGUISTIC PROGRAMMING, SKILLED HELPER MODEL, SOLUTION-FOCUSED and TRANSTHEORETICAL MODEL.

Thus these groupings (though containing more examples) are roughly in line with those put forward by Dryden, but the position of PERSONAL CONSTRUCT THERAPY does not find a clear agreement. I suspect that the deceased founder of this type of therapy, George Kelly,[19] would favour Dryden's judgement over that of Feltham and Horton. But apart from this anomaly, the lists are fairly congruent. Out of the 22 listings of types of therapy in Feltham and Horton only four (NARRATIVE THERAPY, PSYCHODRAMA, NEURO-LINGUISTIC PROGRAMMING and SOLUTION-FOCUSED THERAPY) have clear theoretical origins in, or connections with, family therapy or GENERAL SYSTEMS THEORY to reflect Pentony's contextual model.

The same broad pattern is evident in the *Handbook of Counselling Psychology*, edited by Ray Woolfe, Windy Dryden and Sheelagh Strawbridge.[20] This lists nine 'perspectives on practice': psychodynamic; humanistic; cognitive behavioural; existential-phenomenological; feminist; transpersonal; constructivist; systems; eclectic; and integrative. Again the contextual model ('systems') is in the minority and personal construct therapy is listed separately (dubbed 'constructivist') from the others (as per Dryden) and not incorporated within a cognitive behavioural approach (as per Feltham and Horton). As Dryden is a co-editor, this is not surprising. FEMINIST

THERAPY is mainstreamed in this listing, whereas it is not in the other texts. In Feltham and Horton, it is discussed as a specialism, rather than a mainstream form of therapy.

By this stage I hope that the reader is getting a sense of the recent consensus about the main styles of therapy available. This is not a perfect consensus about what is to be included. Nor are the groupings of approach neatly equivalent but a broad regularity can be seen across the three handbooks. These handbooks suggest that the placebo and resocialisation models, described by Pentony, dominate psychological treatment and the contextual model remains in their shadow.

In line with this marginalisation of the contextual model, the pattern also suggests that professional accounts of therapy remain heavily centred upon individual, especially psychodynamic, treatment. The individual emphasis is also reflected in published *client* accounts of therapy[21] and in advice to clients from professionals about what therapy is on offer.[22] The recent survey of client views of feminist therapy from the Women's Therapy Centre in London also focuses on psychodynamic therapy.[23]

Settings and presenting problems

Whilst the above discussion about classifying therapy according to the therapist's theory, 'model', 'approach' or 'paradigm' is important in any understanding of the nature of psychological treatment, it is defined by other factors as well. I want to return now to those raised in the previous chapter, which are about the *setting* of therapy and the *type of problem* being treated.

The great majority of models of individual therapy were developed in particular settings, which were characterised by voluntarism (at one end of the continuum shown in Figure 1 in Chapter 1, p. 10). At first this was overwhelmingly about private practice. This had a number of implications for the culture of psychological treatment. It had a self-selecting bias towards clients who could afford to pay (maybe extensively if the therapy was intense and lengthy). Thus the models emerging of human dysfunction from therapeutic encounters had a class and racial bias and they generated versions of individual psychology (knowledge centred on inner or 'intra-psychic' events and two-person relationships).

As well as this bias, it also was offered to people who anxiously sought and gratefully received the offer. But in later years, psychological treatments were applied in settings where the patient was less voluntary. This poses an interesting challenge. If client motivation to change and form a therapeutic alliance are important as a starting position for good outcome in therapy, what of those who are less motivated?

Statutory mental health services only slowly began to incorporate talking treatment after the First World War. Moreover, when the Second World War arrived, it became evident that the psychological casualties arriving in the military hospitals were too many to be treated individually. This created conditions of necessity – group therapy had to be invented, Wilfred Bion, a psychoanalyst, being a major contributor.[24] With this came different priorities in model formation (Pentony's rationales for change). These were biased far more towards social influence and opportunities for learning as was noted above. The models generated came from military patients – a different group than, for example, Freud's patients. Indeed, the setting had such a profound influence on psychoanalysts working in groups that they were shocked into making sense of a new world outside of the single-patient mode of practice.[25] Thus, old ways of thinking for the therapist (not the client) had to be abandoned in favour of new ones. I will return to the work of Bion and his colleagues below.

As statutory services began to work with children as well as adults and with families containing more than one 'identified patient', another population emerged which would be the basis for model development. Whereas the artificially convened stranger group could start to work with the power of groups to induce change in its diverse individual members, family therapy started from the premise that the presenting natural group was in some way dysfunctional in its own peculiar right. A variant was that couples can also be dysfunctional and so the target of psychological treatment.[26]

In the 1950s this led to a major divergence between family work and other types of client contact. As was noted above, the contextual model was developed outside the tradition of individual therapy. Even today the best examples of the contextual model are present in the culture of family therapy (in children's services more than in adult mental health services). The attempted transfer of a psychodynamic approach from individuals and groups to family therapy soon gave way to one based more on GENERAL SYSTEMS THEORY.[27] The latter was the explicit theoretical shift that warranted Pentony drawing attention to a separate therapeutic paradigm – the contextual model. Even later forms of family therapy rejecting GENERAL SYSTEMS THEORY (for example POSTMODERN THERAPY approaches) retained a strong contextual emphasis.

Thus, when we try to understand the answer to this chapter's question, we can respond according to four main considerations:

• *The number of clients can define psychological treatment:* This is evident when looking at the different models and emphases in individual, group and family therapy.

• *The type of model can define psychological treatment:* This is evident in the models clustered into placebo, resocialisation and contextual approaches and in the groupings listed in therapy handbooks which fall broadly into psychodynamic, existential and cognitive styles (with hybrids and eclecticism at their boundaries).

• *The type of setting can define psychological treatment:* Clearly the ways of thinking about personal change were different in private individual therapy, soldier-patients corralled into groups and in dysfunctional families seen by statutory services (especially child and adolescent services). Another peculiar setting can be added to this list: forensic work in prisons and secure hospitals.

• *The type of presenting problem being treated can define psychological treatment:* Sometimes presenting problems and the setting they are treated in co-define therapy. An example would be the psychological treatment of substance misuse – where the problem of the client shapes the service purpose ('drug and alcohol services'). At other times, it does not define the setting but we find the type of therapy being linked explicitly to psychiatric diagnosis (e.g. 'cognitive behaviour therapy for anxiety disorders').

These four aspects of understanding about the nature of psychological treatment are reflected in common edited textbooks. For example, Feltham and Horton[28] have separate parts explicitly addressing three of the above. All four are addressed in Stephen Palmer and Gladeana McMahon's *Handbook of Counselling.*[29]

In the previous chapter I drew attention to the continuum of voluntarism. This is correlated strongly with one of the four aspects of treatment (setting). Setting does not preclude any of the models of therapy but does strongly shape how many people are seen at a time and it often is linked to which presenting problems are being treated. Here are some examples of the impact of setting:

• In private practice most clients are already functioning sufficiently well that they can earn enough to pay regular fees. This does not preclude clients being seen with a wide range of personal problems but psychotic patients are very scarce. Private therapists can be found offering individual, group and family therapy.

• In primary care most clients receiving psychological treatment present with 'common neurotic misery', which is often diagnosed as 'depression' or 'anxiety disorders'. Individual counselling is common and group work and computerised therapy less so (though the latter is changing in availability).

• In some state-funded health care systems (like the NHS), specialist outpatient therapy is offered to individuals or families with problems which are considered to be too complex or intractable for treatment in primary care alone. Access to these services (for GP referrers and their patients) is often difficult and long waiting lists are common.

• Both private and state-funded residential services exist which patients enter voluntarily. Examples here would be residential substance misuse rehabilitation services. These tend to combine individual and group therapy. Sometimes they are run on therapeutic community lines (see below).

• Acute psychiatric settings and community mental health teams typically treat psychotic patients using a mixture of drugs and psychosocial interventions. Those with substance misuse and personality problems are also likely to shape the offer of some form of psychological intervention. The challenge for therapists in these settings is how to adapt the assumptions of models of therapy that were developed overwhelmingly in voluntary contexts for use with clients who are involuntary or 'pseudo-voluntary'; (see previous chapter).

- In secure settings where clients overwhelmingly are offender-patients, the challenge of adapting these models with voluntary origins is at its greatest. The notion of 'client' is at its least sustainable here. The term assumes that the identified patient is being 'served' in some sense by staff, when the latter are clearly serving third-party interests (the courts and the general public). I move to the implications of these contradictions now.

Adaptations for the pseudo-voluntary and involuntary patient

I noted above that tensions began to emerge in the twentieth century about models of therapy, which had been created within outpatient private practice, and the constraints and impositions of residential facilities. As I note below, 'moral treatment', an early version of what we now might think of as a 'therapeutic community' approach, was evident on the margins of asylum work. However, the main emphasis in the Victorian system was on the physical management of psychotic patients, who were detained involuntarily (in Britain until 1930 they were all 'certified').

In the first half of the twentieth century little or no psychological rationale was in play about the treatment of psychosis. And in the second half of the twentieth century a strong biological rationale emerged, so that all psychotic patients were simply medicated in an attempt to suppress their symptoms. This led to a clear separation by late in the century (with psychotic patients being treated medicinally and neurotic patients and those with personality problems with psychological treatment).

However, in the early nineteenth century before biological assumptions about madness went into the ascendancy, some (medical and non-medical) reformers, such as Tuke, Browne and Conolly, emphasised that madness was a form of ALIENATION. The argument was that the role of admission was to reduce that social and moral estrangement for inmates. In today's terms these reformers were expressing 'therapeutic optimism' in their commitment to MORAL TREATMENT.

Moral treatment attempted to use social influence to bring the alienated lunatic back into ordinary social intercourse. The parallels between this and the therapeutic community (TC) movement became evident after the Second World War.[30] The pure form of therapeutic communities was developed in two strands in Britain in conditions of warfare. The first applied psychoanalytical ideas to small and large groups of military personnel in residential settings to treat 'war neurosis' (previously 'shellshock' and, today, 'post-traumatic stress disorder'). Above, the work of Wilfred Bion was noted in this context – other psychoanalysts involved in this work were Sigmund Foulkes, Tom Main and John Rickman. These psychoanalysts worked together in the 'Northfield Experiments' at Hollymoor Hospital, Birmingham between 1942 and 1948.

In a second and separate development at Mill Hill, an eclectic approach, which focused more on social learning and education, was developed by Maxwell Jones. After the war, these TC experiments with military patients were extended to NHS hospitals by Tom Main (at the Cassell Hospital) and Maxwell Jones (at Belmont Hospital – the TC unit at Belmont eventually separated out to form the Henderson Hospital). A TC approach was championed further by David Clark, at Fulbourn Hospital.[31]

Today the assumptions of the pure therapeutic community described have been extended (in weakened forms) to other residential facilities. What the therapeutic community 'movement' did, apart from generate new knowledge about how small and large groups can change attitudes and behaviour through peer influence, was highlight that the original private practice model of therapy involving the *voluntary attendance of individuals* was unsustainable in all settings but that other forms of adapted psychological treatments could (or had to) be developed.

The military inmates of Northfield and Mill Hill were pseudo-voluntary patients. War conditions, the directives of military life and the impracticality of individual therapy, because of the numbers involved, had propelled these psychological casualties into a social experiment that was not of their choice. The adaptation to new conditions was thus two sided. On one side was a new type of (non-voluntary) client group. On the other, a new way of conceptualising therapy was necessitated.

What this shift of emphasis from the fee-paying individual to the state-defined client did was alter irrevocably how psychological treatment was to be understood. Moreover, it provided clues about how to apply psychological treatment outside of the confines of voluntary individual outpatient work. The prospect of applying such treatment was now on offer in residential facilities, with clients who did not choose (or maybe were not keen) on the patient role.

Not surprisingly, residential settings where the therapeutic community approach started to develop were varied because the purpose of the settings varied. For example, today, private 'rehab' for substance-misusing rich celebrities and group work with sex offenders in prisons both reflect faint echoes of a TC rationale, even though the client groups are quite different. What they have in common is that the treatment recipients' conduct is offensive to others and the aim of therapy is to use group influence to re-socialise them to comply with law-abiding and rule-following expectations. Louder echoes of the TC movement were also evident in some prison experiments in the 1970s and 1980s (for example at Grendon in England and Barlinnie in Scotland).

The resonances with moral treatment noted earlier are obvious. They are also evident in some self-help initiatives, such as Alcoholics Anonymous. Its whole quasi-religious emphasis is on the personal confessional in a group setting and the use of the latter to encourage and maintain personal change. Probably the most controversial extension of TC ideas was to working with psychotic inpatients. This emerged in the 1960s in England with the work of David Cooper, one of the leaders of British 'anti-psychiatry',[32] and in Italy as the first part in the radical movement to abandon coercive mental health law and close down the asylum system.[33] As with the advocates of moral treatment, these writers were as much interested in the sociological significance of madness as the use of psychological treatment as a technical process.

Finally, if we turn to forensic settings, a number of threads can be detected. One, already mentioned, is the influence of the TC movement in some prison settings. This has focused on those with a diagnosis of antisocial personality disorder committing violent offences, with psychotic prisoners being excluded. An account of the survival or loss of these initiatives in British prisons is given by Woodward.[34]

Another literature about forensic psychotherapy tends to define it wholly as an application of a psychodynamic approach to offenders – 'the offspring of forensic psychiatry and psychoanalytical psychotherapy'.[35] Indeed there is a genre of writing about forensic psychotherapy focusing on individual psychodynamic treatment in prisons, secure hospitals and forensic outpatient clinics, which is virtually silent about the TC movement and group therapy.[36]

More eclectic and empirical studies of psychological treatment for offending suggest that a range of approaches are effective (with reduced recidivism being the desired outcome). The best predictor of success seems to be programme integrity – the consistency of approach used by therapists and the support of that consistency by managers of the organisational context of the treatment.[37]

This end point of judging psychological treatment by its success at ensuring social conformity (in this case, compliance with the law) seems to have brought us quite a way from the third defining feature of psychological treatment: mental health gain for the client. Or has it? In the previous chapter I argued that psychological (or for that matter biological) treatment is about altering conduct, so that deviance defined by others or the self is less evident. In this sense the empirical emphasis on reducing recidivism in forensic settings is not that different from these other judgements of change.

The final point about work in forensic settings is that it exposes the limits of a medical-curative framework for psychological treatment. Take the example of treating sex offenders. Even when therapy 'works' for this group of offenders (which is does overall) it does not 'cure' them one by one. Not only might their antisocial sexual interest remain to various degrees, all that can be said is that a psychological intervention has reduced the probability of reoffending for the group. In other words, the treated group as a whole reoffends less often than an equivalent group of untreated offenders. However, it is not easy to predict which *particular individuals* within the treated group will and will not reoffend.[38] I return to this point in the final chapter of the book.

Reflections on 'what is psychological treatment?'

In this chapter I have summarised a range of elements in the answer to this question. The first summary point is that a tight definition of psychological treatment is hard to come by. The recurring theme of a relationship, using talk, for the betterment of the client is very rough and ready because so many exceptions can be noted.

Second, although so much of the discussions about therapy centre on the model being used, there is much more to answering the question 'what is psychological treatment?' than offering lists of therapeutic models. A more persuasive answer must also include how many clients are present, where the therapy occurs and what type of presenting problem is being treated.

Third, I still find the broad typing of therapy by Pentony (placebo, resocialisation, contextual) a useful aid to finding order in chaos. For now the contextual model is not at the centre of either the professional or lay discourse about therapy – the other two, particularly when applied to individual clients, predominate.

Fourth although, modern psychological treatment can be understood as an offshoot of psychiatry, in ancient times some philosophers already understood that conversation could be used beneficially in response to the woes of people. For example, Albert Ellis was explicitly influenced by STOICISM, especially from the works of the ancient philosophers Epictetus and Marcus Aurelius, when he developed RATIONAL-EMOTIVE THERAPY.[39]

Fifth, although much of the recent history of mainstream forms of therapy emphasise client voluntarism, in the past century a range of forms of psychological treatment have been applied to pseudo-voluntary and involuntary targets. This has extended the domain of psychological treatment from work with neurotic outpatients to work with criminals, drug addicts, those with a diagnosis of personality disorder, and even (at its most controversial) psychotic patients.

Chapter 3
Can psychological treatment be trusted?

> If you don't trust or don't like your therapist, leave them at once. Faith in your therapist is perhaps the single most important indicator of the likely success of therapy.[1]
> *Stuart Sutherland*

> It's good to talk. *Advertisement for British Telecom*

> Talking only makes it worse. *Grafitti, anon*

Introduction

When a client starts therapy they enter a space of inequality in relation to power and dependency. Having a mental health problem is inherently about distress and dysfunction – the person is sad, frightened, confused about themselves and maybe those around them. Clarity of purpose and self-esteem may be nowhere to be seen. By contrast, the person they face is calm, well, confident and in control. This scenario is fine as long as that discrepancy remains benign rather than exploitative. Moreover, that risk of exploitation has nothing to do with the public reputation, training or general effectiveness of the therapist encountered. Effective therapies may contain untrustworthy practitioners. Conversely, a therapist may act with total personal integrity but be ineffective.

As the opening quote from Sutherland indicates, a client's trust in their therapist is a matter of both self-protection and therapeutic optimism or pessimism. Sutherland was a professor of experimental psychology who tried different types of therapy in the wake of his depressive breakdown. His account and that of other clients are useful to read, whether they endorse the experience or criticise it, because they move us beyond the persuasive claims of therapists on the one hand and the complicated deductions from research on the effectiveness of psychotherapy on the other. They give a voice to the recipients of therapy, even if each voice is borne from varying circumstances.[2]

Lessons from psychoanalysis about trust

Our culturally inherited stereotype about therapy is of an analyst seated (so with his feet on the ground) behind a patient who cannot see him, with their feet in the air because they are on a couch. One does much more talking than the other. From the outset this scenario signalled a power differential that aroused anxiety and hostility in the critics of therapy.

The ambivalent friendship between Sigmund Freud and his wayward pupil, the Hungarian analyst Sandor Ferenczi, crystallises for us an enduring dilemma about whether patients should trust therapists. Two matters of dispute between them remain today. The first was about technique and the other was about whether therapists should affirm or challenge the client's experience. With regard to technique, Freud preached neutrality (an austere distance from the patient's life and desires) in order to interpret the TRANSFERENCE (unconscious reactions of the patient to their therapist).

Freud invented the concept of transference initially as a defence manoeuvre *for the therapist* against the raw feelings of love and hate that can arise in intimate relationships. Freud developed this theory about transference when observing the panic and confusion that beset his colleague, Joseph Breuer, when a patient fell in love with him. Although Szasz[3] argues that transference is not *merely* a defence (it can lead to useful interpretive insights for the patient), he also notes that its advantages for the therapist are not in doubt. The therapist can say it is not me that is loved or hated, what is happening is that earlier feelings towards parents are being 'projected' or 'displaced' onto me.

By contrast, Ferenczi moved towards direct honesty with his patients and even experimented with 'mutual analysis', where the patient and therapist switched roles. He believed that the direct affirmation of the therapist's love in the 'real relationship' healed mental distress, and went as far as arguing that interpretation was a sadistic act and that therapy was like rape – a demonstration of power, not care and respect.

The second point of dispute between Freud and Ferenczi was about accounts from survivors of childhood abuse. At first Freud took these at face value, but he changed his mind and began to argue that survivors were reporting fantasised desires not real events from the past. Ferenczi disagreed and opted for Freud's initial stance.

Modern psychodynamic therapists insist that Freud was essentially correct about technique and Ferenzi was wrong for clinical, ethical and legal reasons. For example, Langs argues that where boundary violations occur then the relationship may collapse or it may degenerate into exploitation. Either way, according to Langs, its therapeutic value is lost.[4]

But this recent psychodynamic orthodoxy has not put the matter to rest – far from it. Masson considers that Freud's change of mind about sexual molestation and incest has provided therapists with a catastrophic legacy, particularly now that evidence about the full scale of childhood abuse has come to light.[5] And as far as technique is concerned, the austere neutrality encouraged by Freud triggered so many dissenting reactions, from behaviourism, existentialism and humanism during the twentieth century, that it was not sustained across the culture of therapy. In other words, therapists now are likely to be directive and many cultivate reciprocal honesty as a therapeutic process in its own right. Ferenczi's defiance eventually became a role model for a new version of orthodoxy outside of psychodynamic circles, in which honest directness is valued between clients and therapists.

However, the failure to agree between therapists about the status of survivors' accounts and reciprocity in the therapeutic relationship has posed a stark dilemma for any prospective client. They may find therapists who do not believe their experience or turn it into something else. They may find therapists who remain cruelly aloof. At the other end of the spectrum, to dissolve professional distance may lead to abusive outcomes. What if the therapist wants to share their problems or wants to have a friendship or sex with the client? As for financial exploitation, we have no clear account of how Ferenczi negotiated who paid whom when he moved to 'mutual analysis'.[6] In other words, since the turn of the twentieth century with the Freud–Ferenczi dispute, new versions of uncertainty have been created about clients trusting professionals.

Trust in therapists and trust in therapeutic systems

This focus on the varied *individual* aspects of trust in therapists can be broadened though. Health *systems* may or may not be trusted to provide accessible, acceptable, appropriate and effective therapies in all localities. Private and NHS patients may be part of a postcode lottery for psychological help, as much as for any other form of treatment. As for pseudo-voluntary and involuntary patients, overwhelmingly they get what they are given. Trust in health care is thus multi-layered: interpersonal trust is only one aspect to think about. For psychological treatment though, the interpersonal dimension to trust is particularly important, given the central importance of the relationship in predicting the outcome of therapy.

As became obvious in Chapter 2, the psychological therapies are diverse in nature. Moreover, the preferred approaches to treatment are scattered across the mental health professions. The latter collectively are sometimes called the 'psy complex'. The core of the psy complex includes psychiatrists, clinical psychologists, mental health nurses and social workers or occupational therapists working as specialists in mental health services.

Thus, when a client enters therapy, in public sector health and social care agencies they will encounter practitioners who typically have a double form of training. Usually, in the core of the 'psy complex', this will be in medicine, psychology, nursing or social work, followed by specialist training in one model (sometimes more) of therapy. Thus the practitioner has a dual identity, based first on their original training and then, subsequently on a particular model.

For those in receipt of therapy, this common mixed identity of most therapists is important for three reasons. First, the original discipline of the practitioner has a bearing on the way mental health problems are framed. Second, practitioners tend to have more in common with those from different backgrounds who share their current common model than with those sharing their original professional training. In other words, the identity of the therapist may be governed more by their model of therapy, say, being a psychodynamic psychotherapist, rather than by their background, for example as a psychiatrist or psychologist. Third, forms of accountability for good practice are shaped, to some extent, by membership of two clubs – one based on a core profession and the other on a shared approach to therapy. I want to move to this question of accountability more generally now.

The role of professional membership in promoting good practice

Professional training and membership is relevant to our confidence in any particular therapist for a number of reasons, which accummulate over time:

• The original training of mental health workers helps to ensure that they have a basic and general understanding of people with mental health problems. This gives them some confidence in client engagement and guides them about how to form an appropriate therapeutic relationship (boosting the placebo effect).

• Experience with clients in general casework familiarises the therapist-to-be with clients with a range of problems and enables them to understand how parts of the mental health system work. This is important for them to assess whether clients referred to them are appropriate and whether they should themselves refer on elsewhere, if they consider that they are not competent to deal with the client and their presenting problem. This point about general client contact applies much less to those private practitioners who were trained only as psychotherapists. However, they may still cautiously refer on if and when they feel out of their depth with a client.

• Training in one or more therapeutic models ensures the production of rationales (reasoned explanations) for their work (discussed in chapter 2).

• Supervision during therapy training and subsequently once qualified helps to ensure that therapists act competently and with personal integrity.

• Apart from post-qualification training and supervision (called 'continued professional development' or 'CPD') demanded by professional bodies, members of professional organisations are obliged to subscribe to codes of conduct or ethical codes. These do not guarantee that a therapist acts with personal integrity but they do mean that a client knows that their therapist understands how they *ought* to conduct themselves professionally in their role. It also provides the prospect of an aggrieved client appealing to a professional body if they consider that their therapist has in some way failed them.

Despite the assurances to clients that might flow from the above arguments for properly trained practitioners, it is not inevitable that they always lead to either competence or personal integrity. In other words, we cannot assume for certain that professional training and the regulation of the therapy professions neccesarily ensure good therapeutic relationships for all clients. I return to this matter below when discussing legal regulation.

Employing good practitioners and dealing with failures in care

Therapists are not only guided in their daily work by a combination of original and post-qualification training and supervision, they need to comply with rules of probity (integrity) set down for them. The first framework of these rules has just been noted (ethical codes set out by professional bodies). The second framework is derived from rules of employment. In the case of private practitioners only the first of these frameworks is applicable, though all practitioners are subject to the criminal law, which I discuss below. In public sector health and social care settings, therapists employed have job descriptions and personal specifications. The credentials they claim in their job applications are open to scrutiny by their new employer.

Once employed, grounds for dismissal may include evidence of incompetent or unethical practice. There is not always a neat fit in particular cases though between professional definitions of minimum standards. A practitioner may be disciplined by their professional body but not dismissed from employment. Conversely a practitioner may be dismissed but not be investigated by their professional body. Moreover, in particular cases of errant practice, the quality and efficiency of communication between employers and professional bodies is variable.

Returning to codes of practice, these are the main vehicle for maintaining standards in practice for the following reasons:

- It is assumed that practitioners know what is expected of them from these codes of ethics (I emphasise again here though that this assumption may be unfounded in practice).

- Ethical codes are points of reference for processes that ensure good practice. For example, in the case of therapists, they may be expected to attend for supervision for their work and ensure that they keep up to date with new knowledge and debate.

- Codes of conduct are a point of reference about peer surveillance. An example here is that a practitioner who becomes aware of incompetent or unethical practice in a colleague is duty bound to report them to their professional body.

- In relation to redress for unhappy clients, a code of practice gives the client or their advocate wordings for their grievance – they can cite which rules they consider have been broken from the code.

For governments, employers and clients, who rely on codes of practice as touchstones to monitor standards of practice and deal with rule-breaking, there are a few challenges to their confidence. The first, already mentioned, is that practitioners may not walk around in their daily practice with their professional code as an internal reference point. Whilst ignorance is not a defence, ignorance may nonetheless exist, so the assumed internal reference point for good practice may be missing. The second is that codes are expressed in very general terms and may not address the nuances and complexities of professional–client relationships.

The third is that understandings of failure in care have increasingly addressed organisational or systemic complexity. This tendency to analyse 'adverse' or 'critical' incidents from a systemic rather than individual perspective is at odds with the logic and emphasis of codes of practice. Indeed, the organisational framework for analysing failures of care tends to emphasise the influence of factors above and beyond those apparent in individual circumstances. This framework encourages a low-blame or even no-blame approach. Thus, when care fails there is a contradictory discussion surrounding the failure, which contains a mixture of high and low blame. The aggrieved client will find themselves facing the mixed messages arising from this ambivalent professional and organisational culture.

I refer the reader to Stone[7] for a fuller discussion of the role of codes of practice in claiming to enhance client protection and to Price[8] about the move from individual culpability to an emphasis on system failure in legal measures aimed at protecting the public. I now turn to the use of the law.

The legal context of good practice

Broadly there are two forms of legislation that are intended to protect clients: one focuses specifically on the regulation of health care professions and practices and the other on aspects of the criminal law. In the latter regard, abusive practice (for example physical assaults on, or sexual contact with, clients) potentially can be dealt with under criminal prosecution. For example, in Britain law exists that could be the basis of prosecution by the police of therapists found to have had sexual relationships with their clients (the Sexual Offences Act, 2003). In the USA a minority of states have dedicated legislation which criminalises sexual contact with clients.[9] However, these legal measures are not commonly used.

By contrast to these infrequently used and patchy forms of legislation, it is commonplace for countries to provide a legal framework for the regulation of professions or procedures. The latter distinction is important. For example, generally it is *named professions* which are regulated and much less frequently their particular practices. This is a legal framework to formalise and endorse the assumptions I listed above about ensuring the advantages of professional training and their ethical intentions.

Whether these measures are *effective* is a different matter. The assumption though, which tends to appeal to our immediate common sense, is that legally recognised professions are going to be more competent and ethical than unregulated practitioners. Whether we are correct to trust our common sense about this matter boils down to a question: in practice, does regulation reduce risk to clients and make therapists more trustworthy? To my knowledge, we simply do not know the answer to this question and yet all of those who are strongly demanding state regulation as an effective mechanism to raise levels of trust and minimise risk assert that their policy is effective in practice.

In recent times, a web of legal measures has been introduced in the UK, which is more elaborate than those focusing on professional regulation alone. For example, in statutory services (and often in the voluntary sector) providers must comply with legal measures to protect children and vulnerable adults. Particular laws (the 1999 Protection of Children Act; the 2000 Care Standards Act; and the 2001 Health and Social Care Act) demand that employers deploy pre-employment police checks on new recruits.

Legal frameworks of professional state registration spell out explicit rules about: (i) the type and levels of training which indicate practitioner competence; and (ii) accountability measures available to aggrieved clients if practitioners are found to be in breach of codes of conduct. The logic here is that legal regulation gives clients access to appropriately trained practitioners who are governed by transparent complaints procedures, which will mete out justice.

General arguments for and against legal registration

If effective, legal registration ensures that the public has access to a transparent and legally legitimate means to bring errant practitioners to book. And when practitioners are then held to account it is assumed that the outcome will be fair to both parties. That is, the unfairly accused practitioner will be vindicated and then left free to practise and the fairly accused will receive forms of punishments that are proportionate to their misdeeds. Politicians and professional bodies are generally in favour of this logic. In the case of politicians they are keen to indicate to their voters that government power can be exercised to protect the public good. This emotional appeal is particularly strong when the public is vulnerable (when they are sick or disabled).

If legal registration is a high-sounding moral platform for politicians about their ability to protect the vulnerable citizen, for professionals much more is at stake. By campaigning for and achieving mechanisms of legal registration they are also involved in a process of professional advancement. Professionals gain important advantages for themselves without reference to the explicit aim of client protection. Regulated professionals can claim a higher status in the marketplace than those who are unregulated.

In the sociology of the professions, these advantages of state recognition are referred to as 'social closure'. Regulation is a central mechanism for professionals to maintain their tribal boundary by monopolising a form of knowledge and rendering it scarce. Others (clients and competing professions) are excluded from this knowledge.[10] It is a route to power over others. It offers special status to the group and it can be a justification for employment rights and bids for raised salary levels or fees for service.

Social closure relies on two main processes: control over entrance to a profession via selection for training; and state recognition of the profession's unique qualities via legal registration. It represents the successful engagement of a particular professional group and the state leading to a legal arrangement in which both benefit.[11]

With these thoughts in mind about what professionals are up to, critics of registration argue that there is a hidden agenda – practitioners are not being altruistic when they argue for registration on grounds of client protection. But if professionals can be accused of duplicity in this regard, the simple question of the *effectiveness* of legal regulation remains an important one. This is an empirical question, which is separate from the question about motives for seeking social closure.

Specific arguments about psychological treatment
Therapists usually have a dual group membership, as I noted earlier. A few therapists are trained only in one model and have no original training in the mental health professions – sometimes this is called having 'direct entry' to the profession of psychotherapy. With regard to dual membership, all of the mental health professions are regulated in most developed countries. There are differences though in the degree to which each nation-state grants autonomy about keeping a professional register.

In some cases the professions self-regulate and they keep their own register of practitioners with the state's blessing. In other cases, the register is held by an independent authority. In Britain there are now moves to shift towards the latter system for all the professional groups under new legal arrangements to cover all health care professionals. This arrangement would cover the core mental health professions that practise psychotherapy in its various forms (but not those seeking 'direct entry'). The latter therapists are those whose basis for practice is being trained in one model of therapy and who hold *no other prior credentials* as mental health workers (such as being a clinical psychologist or mental health nurse). For this reason, historically, those with such prior credentials, who practise forms of therapy, have not been as keen or interested in psychotherapy per se being legally regulated as the direct entry therapists. They point to the more general legal and organisational arrangements about registered practice in their *core profession* to demonstrate their fitness to practise.

This tension, between the core-trained and the direct-entry practitioners, is highlighted by the registration of psychotherapy debate in Britain. In the early 1970s the Church of Scientology, which promotes a particular form of therapy called 'dianetics', attempted to infiltrate the largest mental health charity in Britain, MIND. This triggered an official inquiry (the Foster Report, 1971), which recommended that there should be state registration of psychotherapy. This recommendation lay fallow and a number of private therapy organisations lobbied the government to implement the Foster advice.

Another review requested by government (the Seighart Report, 1978) also suggested the need to regulate psychotherapy. However, clinical psychologists demanded instead that *psychologists* (not therapists) should have a statutory register. This led to a ten-year campaign from the British Psychological Society to secure its own register of

'Chartered Psychologists'. Moreover, psychologists replayed their bid for a monopoly over bids for registration when they established their own register of psychologists with a special interest in psychotherapy in 2001 within the British Psychological Society.

In the meantime, moves to register psychotherapy had run into the sands. During the 1980s and 1990s all the different groups of therapists debated ways and means of developing a common position in relation to registration, within a loose body of affiliation called the 'United Kingdom Council for Psychotherapy'. Such a united front was always a long shot given the highly variegated nature of the trade (see Chapter 2). How could a common language be developed? Could the different factions even agree on what psychological knowledge was? An irony of this failure to agree was that all the evidence about personal change indicates that models or rationales are less important than the quality of human relationships (a point that therapists from different stables generally agree on privately). And yet the negotiation about the common front was being conducted by representatives of self-regarding organisations, which defined themselves overwhelmingly by their preferred models.

The attitude of groups dominated by independent practitioners (largely working outside the state sector and usually without a core disciplinary training) shifted from the 1970s, when registration was seen as an opportunity (between the Foster and Seighart Reports). Now registration is seen as a threat to independent practice, as can be seen from the following petition from that sector about the emerging framework for regulating the health professions in 2007. This statement is taken from the website of Ipnosis which represents the interests of this sector in Britain:[12]

STATEMENT OF OPPOSITION TO THE STATE REGULATION OF PSYCHOTHERAPY, COUNSELLING AND PSYCHOANALYSIS

There are many reasons for opposing the state regulation of the psychological therapies, among the range of arguments are the following:

1. No reputable or systematic research exists to demonstrate that counsellors, psychotherapists and psychoanalysts abuse or exploit clients on a scale that warrants the costs (financial, political, cultural and psychological) of state regulation.

2. The medicalised framing of current regulation proposals violates the public's right to choose practitioners who do not define them as patients suffering from illnesses or disorders, and who offer a rich variety of other models for human wellbeing and development.

3. Given the lack of evidence that regulation will effectively protect the public, it is difficult not to conclude that training and accrediting organizations have been promoting state regulation because it enables them to market state validation as an exclusive passport into practice, in turn justifying rising training costs and ever higher academic attainment as key criteria for acceptance into training.

4. Existing research suggests a) that good therapeutic outcomes are not demonstrably related to levels or types of training; b) that good outcomes are strongly correlated with the successful creation of an effective helping relationship between practitioner and client.

5. Regulation based on training falsely promises that training guarantees good practice, and reliance on this unwarranted view in turn misleads the public: the ability to achieve good results ultimately counts for more than the level of training

achieved, and this can only be effectively monitored through client feedback, supervision, case seminars and ongoing peer review.

6. A centralised monoculture of psychological regulation, gridlocking therapy into standardised training, competency and ethical criteria, is intrinsically inferior to the current diverse and appropriately local ecologies of psychological service provision. This rich diversity of the psychological therapies is a precious and desirable phenomenon.

7. It is not the proper business of the state to control the provision of counselling, psychotherapy and psychoanalysis. Such control can never be apolitical. State regulation of psychological therapies will compromise practitioner neutrality, lead to risk-averse practice and erode the client's freedom of choice.

State regulation will install a terminally damaging confusion of ends and means. If the end need is for 'client protection' the damage done to services delivered to clients by means of occupations that are statutorily regulated is likely to overwhelmingly outweigh any enhancement of their interests that might ensue.

Since psychopractice is ultimately a form of conversation between consenting others, the creation, funding, and enhancement of service-user education and information would be far more cost effective and beneficial to users than state regulation, which will be ineffective in minimizing abuse or exploitation.

For some or all of these reasons amongst others – all of which have been argued and evidenced at length elsewhere – we, the undersigned, are of the opinion that the government should relinquish any intention statutorily to regulate the fields of counselling, psychotherapy, and psychoanalysis.

The arguments in the above Statement are useful to consider. I personally agree with some and not others. For example, the argument about limited abuse in therapy suggests that those opposed to registration can be as suspect in their reasoning as those promoting it – I return to the evidence about therapy as danger in the next chapter. Also, what the petition calls 'psychopractice' is not always a 'conversation between consenting others' – I keep reminding the reader that psychological treatment is often offered and received by pseudo-voluntary and involuntary clients. But the point of including the list here is not to uncritically endorse it or select points I disagree with. Instead I use it to highlight the inherent complexity and controversy about trying to legislate for good professional practice.

Now that the professionalising efforts of psychologists and therapists have been outlined and objections to it also listed, where is the evidence that registration of either or both would lead to greater public protection? The answer is that to date, that evidence is missing. What we do know though is that those who are already qualified and on a voluntary rather than statutory register may be treated leniently by professional bodies.

For example, in 1998 a prestigious clinical psychologist, Professor Peter Slade, from the University of Liverpool, was disciplined for his serial sexual abuse of patients. However, he was not expelled from the British Psychological Society and he was only asked voluntarily to remove himself from the register and to undertake to desist from patient contact. Many inside and outside the profession considered this to be extremely lenient. And those who took this critical view emphasised the damaging signal this leniency gave to the public about which interests professionals prioritised (i.e. their own, not their clients).

Moreover, in the case of the medical profession, where there has been a longstanding established state register and self-regulation has been accepted by government, public confidence has declined not increased. As has been noted, cultural shifts about patient autonomy, public scepticism about traditional expertise and an increasing emphasis on risk assessment and management have brought the profession into regular question.[13]

Two low points came at the turn of this century for British medicine with the discovery that a GP, Harold Shipman, had murdered many of his elderly patients, and that heart surgeons at Bristol Royal Infirmary had whimsically researched infant cardiac surgery with innumerable deaths ensuing. Critical investigations of the profession's own efforts at investigation (the General Medical Council) revealed a bias towards self-protection, rather than justice for patients and their relatives failed by medical malpractice.[14] For example, the general public commonly believed that discredited doctors, once removed from the medical register, would not practice again. However, most erasures are temporary, with recommendations being about periods of support, close supervision and re-training.

All of this gives good grounds for the public to distrust professionals. But it also leads to a paradoxical political outcome – the answer offered by government and the professions to a crisis of public confidence in the professions is more regulation. The paradox is that registration is well tested (at least in relation to the older professions like medicine) and has been found lacking. And the Slade example given above shows that formal professional legitimacy (being a well-trained senior registered practitioner) offered no public protection. The weak punitive response from his professional body, along with the fact that he was *already* on a register, do not inspire public confidence in the 'more of the same' formula about legal registration protecting clients.

A final point I would make about the registration of therapy debate is that, for now, it is being swept along with the wider government push to regulate *professions not practices*. To date very few laws specify or define forms of practice (rather than broad professional labels like 'medical practitioner'). Exceptions in Britain are the 1984 Dentists Act (about operating on teeth) and the 1997 Nurses, Midwives and Health Visitors Act (about delivering babies).[15] For the time being, if legal registration is to offer any protection for the public (and I emphasise this supposed protection has still to be clearly demonstrated), it will not be about the direct regulation of therapy. Instead it will come indirectly from the therapist's affiliation with a particular health profession.

Last reflections

The above outlines the layers of reassurance given to the public about the trustworthiness of therapists. Together these increase the chances of clients encountering competent and respectable practitioners. They do not guarantee this desired outcome – they only increase the probability of it being met. A practitioner may be well intentioned but not very good. Thus, there is an important difference between us trusting intentions and trusting competence in a service provider. To complicate matters further, a practitioner may be competent with some clients but let others down. In other words, the layers of accountability outlined in this chapter increase a client's luck but they do not guarantee a satisfactory outcome.

From a voluntary client perspective, therapy is not a complete roulette. There is information available to guide their decisions about 'best bets'. However, the client has to be in a position to exercise voluntary choice and they have to have access to relevant information.

If a client is in a position to exercise some choice over their therapist and their approach, what information is relevant to them? The first sort is addressed in the next chapter and refers to a fundamental question about personal and maybe financial investment. The second challenge is about sourcing information about therapies and therapists. In the Appendix to this book (p. 123) the public can find organisations for this purpose. The third challenge comes after the event – what if a client is unhappy with the therapy they have embarked upon for some reason?

The discussion in this chapter suggests that despite layers of potential protection from the outcomes of professional training, rules of employment, codes of practice and legal registration, clients, both individually and collectively, remain vulnerable when faced with professional power. The only way to eliminate our negative risk at the hands of professionals is to avoid contact with them.[16] This may seem rather drastic but it would work as a risk management strategy. However, that very avoidance also means that the client-to-be is not enjoying the positive risk of seeking and finding an effective and trustworthy practitioner (probably the bulk of those in practice). To avoid therapy completely is a bit like never travelling – it may be safer to stay at home but you then never get to see alternative scenery.

My final reflection in this chapter is that the question of trust in practitioners has two main levels. The first and obvious one for the client is about the chances of trust in a particular therapist being well founded, at a point in their life when they are in need of help. The second is whether all potential clients ('the public') can trust the communities of interest (particularly politicians and professional bodies representing therapists) who offer general formulae for trusting practitioners. These are both a challenge.

On the first count, a client can increase their luck (by means I discussed earlier in the chapter about weighing up information) but there are no copper-bottomed guarantees. Only by trying the relationship will they discover whether this particular therapist is effective and will act in their interests. On the second count, the problem is that there is a tendency for politicians and professional leaders to overstate claims for their own rhetorical advantage, putting trust from potential clients at risk.

For example, blanket legal and bureaucratic mechanisms may or may not reduce risk overall. Moreover, even if they do reduce average risk, they will never *eliminate all* risk and so the client still has to fall back on taking the first type of chance just noted: 'Can I trust this particular person to help me with the particular problems I have in my life at present'. If the public believes that the registration of therapists and legal mechanisms to protect vulnerable people in society will eliminate all risk but then they find themselves let down or abused, then their trust in the advocates of laws and bureaucratic procedures will be undermined.

My view is that *because* there are no guarantees for particular clients with particular therapists and *because* blanket measures from professionalisers and politicians tend towards hyperbole in their promises of protection, we need to keep an open and very public discussion going about risk and trust. This demand for democratic openness and scepticism has been made at some length by Celia Davies and so I refer the interested reader to her work.[17] She argues that we should not naïvely trust professionals but rather than abandon the advantages they offer the public most of the time, we should explore multiple ways of improving confidence via a range of mechanisms. The latter include changes in education and training, mediation, consensus conferences and citizens' juries. All of these are directed towards stakeholder empowerment and consensus-building between providers and their clientele.

Chapter 4
Is psychological treatment worth the investment?

> The way to alleviate and mitigate distress is for us to take care of the world and the other people in it, not to treat them ... [1]
> *David Smail*

> Granted all that is wrong with the mental health movement, the contemporary therapy cults, the helping professions and the social security bureaucracies, most Europeans and Americans may still be suffering more from a lack of what these have to offer than from an overdose. [2]
> *Abram de Swann*

Introduction

In the main, quite properly, this chapter's title question centres on the effectiveness of therapy. However, there is more than this involved if we are to appraise its role more generally in modern society. The latter contains many 'products' that are desired in their own right – it may be that therapy is one of those and some of the time without reference to its effectiveness. Thus if we start with a very broad question about the worthiness of therapy it is soon obvious that it is quite complicated.

In this chapter I deal with this complexity by looking first at our earlier discussion of the range of people and their problems that are treated psychologically rather than just medicinally. I move then to the interesting debate about defining service quality and then have a section looking specifically at effectiveness. From this the various methodological arguments about research into therapy are outlined. The next section looks at those who have argued in principle against providing and accessing psychological treatment. Finally I summarise some points from social science about the role of therapy in society. By the end of this, the reader should have a feel for the subtleties of the question in the chapter's title and offer their own answer or answers.

A reminder of the range of problems treated

To start the discussion I want to return to a theme that I raised earlier about the target of treatment. I introduced the idea of a continuum of coercion in Chapter 1. It became evident in subsequent discussion that psychological treatment is applied to four broad types of psychological problem:

- There are people who feel troubled and seek clarification about and comfort for their woes. Treatment for them is 'anxiously sought and gratefully received'. They are looking for existential exploration or 'personal growth' with a trustworthy stranger. Most of this work occurs in private consultations.

- There are people who consult their GP and are identified as having a 'mild to moderate' mental health problem. Their undifferentiated misery is codified medically as 'depression' or a form of 'anxiety disorder' or 'stress reaction'. They are offered antidepressant medication and/or a form of psychological treatment. The latter takes place (sooner or later, because long waiting lists are common) in primary care or in an outpatient clinic of a psychology or psychotherapy service. They attend voluntarily.

• There are those whose diagnosis is of a 'major mental disorder' or 'serious mental illness'. These are overwhelmingly treated medicinally in specialist mental health services with high rates of compulsion involved. A special form of lawful detention ('sectioning' in the UK) is used by health professionals in the latter. Many of these patients are deemed to be psychotic with diagnoses of 'schizophrenia' or 'bipolar disorder'. A minority of these are given some form of psychological treatment. If they are considered to 'have' a personality disorder or this diagnosis is given with another ('dual diagnosis' or 'co-morbidity') then they are likely to be referred eventually for psychological help. They are considered by professionals to be 'complex cases'. They may accept the offer of psychological treatment more or less enthusiastically. What drives the investment of state services in this group of patients overwhelmingly is the risk to others (in terms of nuisance or actual danger). However, often there is also a real enough paternalistic concern, as well, of a risk to self.

• Finally, there are those who have demonstrably been a risk to others. These are offender-patients in medium and maximum security psychiatric hospitals, or mentally disordered prisoners. In the latter group, apart from some psychotic patients, are those with a diagnosis of 'antisocial personality disorder'. This is invoked by dint of the ruthless antisocial acts committed: rape, child molestation, homicide or grievous bodily harm. These violent and/or sexual offenders may be offered some form of psychological treatment. Unlike the previous group where 'risk to self or others' is at issue, in this forensic group *risk to others* drives professional decision-making at all times.

Thus it can be seen that there is a wide range of psychological problems that psychological treatment is applied to, with much ambiguity in that range of the interests being served. For this reason there are some, like Szasz, who argue that the use of psychotherapy is only justified at the voluntary end of the spectrum. He goes as far as arguing that only fee-paying clients will be able to protect that sacrosanct state of voluntarism.

It is certainly true that having money is a way of protecting one's choice and citizenship. But this protection is not total. For example, clients may be financially exploited by ineffective therapists. And fee-paying voluntary clients are still at the mercy of what is available in their local therapy market and the approach used by their therapist is under the control of the latter. This discrepancy of knowledge creates an imbalance of power from the outset. Szasz is naïve to assume that consumerism protects clients in healing interventions. Much of the knowledge about the latter is derived from professional research and complex ideological assumptions developed over time and place, which are bound up with professional interests and factionalism. This complexity is not even within the full grasp of an individual therapist, let alone their client, to reflect on in this particular relationship, in this time and in this place.

Even if we agree with purists like Szasz in their objections to those who cannot pay having their problems medicalised and treated further along the continuum of coercion, that continuum exists so we can ask questions about the role within it of psychological treatment. I now move to some of these questions.

Assessing the quality of psychological treatment

I noted earlier that effectiveness is the usual topic of discussion in relation to personal or state investment in any form of health intervention (not just psychological treatment). However, it is one of several dimensions to consider when we think about the *quality* of a service to patients. One easily understood and commonly used framework is that of Donabedian.[3] He suggests that a 6 x 3 framework captures all of the main questions we need to ask about service quality (Table 4.1).

Table 4.1 *Donabedian's Framework*

	Structure	Process	Outcome
Accessibility			
Acceptability			
Appropriateness			
Equity			
Effectiveness			
Efficiency			

The first column, 'Structure', refers to *what* is present in a service (typically described in terms of its staff and buildings). Arguments then occur about 'service capacity' – for example, are there enough staff to do the job of meeting demand? The second column is about *how* the service is delivered – the procedures offered to, and the type of relationships with, clients. The third column refers to *patient improvements* – did they get better according to their self-reported symptoms or professionally assessed changes?

The six dimensions then form boxes with the columns and we can insert relevant questions in each box. Is the service easily accessible to clients? Is the service acceptable to the client? Is the service appropriate for their needs? This dimension is particularly contentious, especially in relation to psychological needs. Are the latter defined by the patient or by others?

Thus the first three dimensions (the three 'A' dimensions) are then joined by the three 'E' dimensions. Is there equity of distribution of the service – to what extent is it available to all comers? Is it clinically effective? Is it cost effective? The last of these is usually called 'efficiency' to indicate that a service, or procedure within in it, may be of proven effectiveness but may not be the cheapest option. If two services or procedures are of equal clinical effectiveness then the cheaper of the two is the more efficient.

The reader can place their own questions in each box to test out the quality of service that they have had experience of or know about in their locality. If we now take the four main groupings of patients I noted earlier we can see that they can be mapped on to this framework creating a range of results.

One of the problems we have is that all the questions we might legitimately ask in each box are not answered yet by research – many remain intriguing questions. Also the definition of the elements of quality that Donabedian lays out can be contested. For example, who decides what is 'appropriate'? And what if professionals consider their work to be reasonable and acceptable but patients consider it unacceptable? As I noted above, much of these debates centre on the gap that occurs sometimes between expressed need and defined need – what patients want and what professionals think that they should have.

Donabedian's table is a very good framework for discussion and service audit purposes but definitions of the six dimensions are open to debate. However, it provides a common framework to have those debates. An implication of Donabedian's model of quality, from a patient perspective, is that an optimal service is one in which a high rating is obvious in all six outcome boxes. (Of course a blinkered or self-centred patient might ignore the equity and efficiency dimensions and limit their interest to the quality of their own therapy.)

Generally professionals would agree with the emphasis on the six outcomes but, as politicians know, all too often they tend to start with, and sometimes limit their demands to, the structure boxes – they special plead for resources for their profession (more posts, more accommodation and more money). In recent years this history of special pleading has been countered by policy makers being interested in the relationship between process and outcome or, even more narrowly, outcomes alone. Policy makers, for obvious reasons, are also keen to shift the focus from effectiveness to cost-effectiveness (efficiency).[4]

Having argued that we can consider quality in broader terms than effectiveness and efficiency, I now turn to them, as they are at the centre of the critical question forming the heading for this chapter.

Effectiveness and efficiency

Good summaries of the evidence about effectiveness can be found in Barkham (2007) and Bower and Barkham (2006).[5] Evidence refers to the findings of randomised controlled trials (RCTs). An RCT is a trial consisting of two randomly assigned groups of people with comparable characteristics, one group being offered treatment, in this case therapy, the other being the control, or placebo group, who are offered an intervention not considered to be an active rationale for personal change. Note that waiting list controls are different from this – in true placebo conditions some form of neutral personal contact is ensured for the same duration as the wing of the trial which contains the therapy under investigation.

In the case of drug trials, the randomisation can be 'double-blind' (neither the professional nor the patient knows what treatment is being given). Clearly this is not possible in psychological treatment because the therapist must know what they are offering in the relationship. With this inherent methodological difficulty in mind, the main message from these reviews can be summarised as follows:

• Both treatment and placebo are better than no treatment. The superiority of the placebo group in randomised controlled trials to no treatment reminds us of the argument for the placebo model discussed in Chapter 2.

• When therapies of different orientation are compared, there appear to be few differences between them in effectiveness. Again this supports the placebo model. It is also consistent with the early finding of Yates,[6] when studying behavioural techniques (the latter can be radically altered in content and yet effective outcomes still ensue).

• There is some evidence that some presenting problems are better treated using particular methods. For example, anxiety symptoms are most efficiently treated with behavioural and cognitive behavioural therapies than with exploratory psychotherapy.[7]

Barkham notes that research in the area developed in terms of four steps over time (or 'generations') to create the above recent summary picture.[8] First generation research studied whether therapy overall was efficacious and to what extent. The second generation addressed a question summed up by Paul: 'What treatment, by whom, is most effective for this individual with that specific problem and under which set of circumstances?'[9] Third generation research focuses on cost-effectiveness or service efficiency. The fourth generation moved towards addressing client reported improvement in actual services – what Barkham calls 'clinically meaningful outcome research'. This point is picked up again below when discussing the Seligman Report.[10]

The three bulleted points above about treatment effectiveness summarise a current overall picture. However, cautions and commentaries rehearsed from a variety of parties are worth examining, because they give us a more elaborate picture of the complexity of appraising evidence about psychological treatment. Below I divide these wide-ranging reactions about the worth and worthiness of psychological treatment into three types for convenience. They are grouped into those that emphasise methodological points, those that reflect queries in principle to therapy and finally to the way that therapy has been discussed in the literature of social science.

Methodological points and queries

Given the complexity of the field it is not surprising that it has been the subject of much debate. Below I summarise the main points debated.

The empiricist objection

This refers to those who agree with the logic of RCTs to appraise the worth of therapies but point out that we are ignorant of so many aspects of therapy and so, on grounds of financial probity, we should only specifically support those with a clear evidence base.[11] For example, because it is technique-based rather than process-based, CBT is relatively easy to research and so has led to more findings than for other forms of therapy. The same point could be made in a forensic setting about the treatment of sex offenders using cognitive therapy.[12]

But, as Bower and Barkham note, rather than abandon untested therapies, we should really do more research on them.[13] This point is especially relevant in the light of the strong placebo findings and the lack of clear overall differences of effectiveness when different therapies are compared, noted above. Current moves in the UK to 'improve access to psychological therapies' run the risk of narrowly defining them by models like CBT, which are easily researched *as if* they are drug treatments in RCTs. This limits talking treatments to one version on the supply side (therapy services). On the demand side (clients), there is a diverse population with diverse expressed needs about the type of therapy they prefer, so what if they want something other than CBT?

Also, note how evidence-based practice in this context refers to evidence about effectiveness of models and is without reference to the strong evidence about the therapeutic alliance (the quality of the relationship). The latter is a separate and more important guide from research. One of the harshest empiricist critics, Edward Erwin, points out that there is consistent evidence that therapy outperforms untreated groups on waiting lists.[14] However, it does not persuasively outperform placebo groups in RCTs.

Another confirmatory finding for the placebo model is that therapists vary in their effectiveness, within the same treatment approach. This cautions us against focusing unduly on the model and reminds us that the *quality of the relationship* recurs as a central feature of all forms of therapy, affecting outcomes.[15] As even the harsh critic Erwin concludes, particular rationales may be overstated or even unpersuasive but the ordinary qualities of warmth and care, to be found in good practitioners across therapeutic models, ensure that all therapy can 'still do good'.[16] Erwin puts therapy in the same position now as physical medicine was in a century ago, when physicians and lay healers were probably equally effective but the professionals were just beginning to discover how to develop a scientific approach to their trade.

The anti-empiricist objection

This comes from those who argue that there is a limit to how much we can study relationships using traditional scientific methods,[17] and the adequacy of studying techniques in the light of the complexity of patients' personal and social circumstances.[18] This argument is at its strongest in relation to the contradictory outcomes that can occur when therapy is judged by its existential, rather than symptom, outcome. For example, a person who begins to understand themselves better and is honestly facing their particular life circumstances may become *more distressed* than before therapy. Does this indicate that the therapy is working or not? The answer given depends on one's world-view.

The pros and cons of efficacy studies

In the therapy research literature there are two types of study of outcomes. The first (the 'efficacy study') is the ideal type RCT study. It involves: random assignment of patients to treatment and control conditions; the controls contain true placebo elements (not just waiting-list controls); fidelity to treatment models are assured by operational manuals; patients are seen for a fixed number of sessions; target symptoms are specified; raters of improvement are blind to which group the patient is assigned to; those with more than one diagnosis are excluded; and the patients are followed up at a set period of time.

As Seligman points out, much on this wish list bears little relationship to actual services, where treatments are applied in practice. He argues instead that what is traditionally relegated to an inferior or second-best type of study (the 'effectiveness study') should be trusted more.[19] Effectiveness studies examine how treatments fare in real services, where many elements on the wish list for true efficacy studies are missing. In practice treatments vary in their duration. Therapists may switch approaches on pragmatic grounds, rather than sticking dutifully to one approach. Patients may play an active role in choosing or requesting therapy – they are not necessarily passive recipients. Patients often have multiple presenting problems and their symptom profile may change over time. Patients and therapists are often more interested in improvements in overall functioning than in symptom checklists.

Seligman goes on to commend the findings of the *Consumer Reports Survey* in the USA, which included a section on mental health. Of 180,000 invitations, 22,000 answered this section in detail about what they had experienced when they had had a mental health problem in the previous three years for which they had sought help. The level of improvement reported was higher than in efficacy studies. Long-term therapy fared better than short-term therapy and specialists seemed to get more improvement than non-specialists. However, some self-help traditions (like Alcoholics Anonymous) were particularly effective. 'Active shoppers' improved more than passive recipients. No particular mode of therapy seemed superior to any other.

Limited client samples

When we conclude that psychological treatment is or is not effective, these judgements are based upon uneven sampling of the global population. We know more about women's mental health problems than men.[20] Women consult more in primary care and they attend for outpatient psychotherapy more frequently than men. We know most about those with mild to moderate problems in developed countries receiving psychological treatment. We know an increasing amount about psychotic patients and those with a diagnosis of personality disorder.

But huge populations in the world have never had access to forms of therapy developed in Western Europe and North America, which is also true of poorer populations within the latter. Moreover, when these methods begin to be exported elsewhere we encounter differences in cultures about acceptable healing practices and even about the terms used for distress. For example in the latter regard some cultures have no term for 'depression'[21] and yet a 'pandemic' of depression has been identified by the World Health Organization.[22] In the West this has created an understandable debate about whether Eurocentric models of therapy are appropriate for multi-ethnic communities.[23]

The caution about outcomes being studied

The four groupings of recipients noted earlier remind us that the 'point' of therapy varies from context to context. The outcomes to be listed across the continuum of coercion include: personal growth or existential insight; the reduction of distress and the increase in personal confidence in everyday life; the reduction of risk to self; the reduction of risk to others. Thus any overall conclusions about the effectiveness of psychological treatment must take these different contexts and their implied preferred outcomes into consideration. Lambert, Ogles and Masters suggest an inclusive framework for outcomes examining three domains of functioning: intrapersonal outcomes (improvements in thoughts, feelings and action); improved interpersonal relationships; and improved social functioning.[24]

The balance of emphasis of these will vary across the four broad client groups I describe. For example, the ultimate determinant of success in the treatment of sex offenders is that they do not reoffend. Their social functioning is by far the dominant indicator. There is little point in them improving intra- and interpersonally if they still break the law. By contrast, the depressed patient in primary care can be judged by improvements in all three domains.

The paradoxical importance of treatment fidelity

One paradox in outcome research is that although the empiricist critique noted above emphasises the lack of evidence that therapy outperforms placebo, the rationale offered may still have a positive function in practice. The reason for this is that in research trials the consistency of approach is ensured and the therapists are under scrutiny. This consistency is called 'treatment fidelity' or 'treatment integrity' in the professional literature. The research conditions that ensure treatment fidelity mean that, in line with the placebo model discussed in Chapter 2, therapists are likely to act with confidence and personal integrity in research trials. This guarantee cannot be given in practice.

Therapists in practice may vary in their confidence and coherence in their approach and at times they may act in an unhelpful or even harmful way. However, despite these vulnerabilities of actual services, some argue that they generate more optimistic findings about therapeutic outcomes than efficacy trials (see previous point in relation to Seligman's analysis).

The biased focus on individual therapy

The debates about the effectiveness of therapy remain fixated on the individual mode of treatment. Much less has been studied in relation to group, marital and family therapy and approaches to them. This pattern confirms my observations in Chapter 2. It culminates in most of the research resolving the competing claims of Pentony's placebo and resocialisation models, leaving the contextual model, if not out in the cold, certainly as a minority interest. The irony of this is that ultimately the nature of personal change can only be fully understood if the open system and context-specific emphasis favoured by family therapists is taken into account.

Although the number of studies on outcome for family therapy is less than for the individual mode, there is evidence that it is as effective as individual therapy and in some cases it is more *cost-effective*.[25] As with individual therapy there is no evidence of any difference in effectiveness between the models of family therapy studied.

Peoples' lives are complicated and their circumstances and relationships are always changing. Therapists only join into a part of their clients' lived experiences. This point has important implications for the placebo effect in two senses. First, therapists are only one of many potential inputs to psychological well-being. Extra-therapeutic relationships operate for good or bad in families, friendship networks, work contexts and neighbourhoods. Second, it highlights that these multiple influences are operating on a waiting list: the latter is not some sort of laboratory-style, experimentally static closed system comparison for therapy.

In one of the earliest empiricist attacks on psychotherapy Eysenck noted what he called 'spontaneous remission' – some patients improve if nothing is offered.[26] But of course something may not be offered but something is always happening in people's lives. Their relationships are in flux and their constructions about their lives change over time, independent of professional input. To state the obvious, just as life circumstances create the conditions under which mental health can deteriorate, they might also create the conditions under which it might improve. These life circumstances are an open system, which therapy may or may not become part of for varying amounts of time.

The notion of 'spontaneous remission' has the same mystical quality as 'spontaneous combustion'. Problems do not 'spontaneously remit' in this mystical sense – mental health changes, for good or bad, because of complex life circumstances and reflections on them. This point has become more evident as the interest in mental health gain has shifted away at times from therapy and towards self-help. In the latter, life worlds are compared in an unvarnished way and opportunities for peer empathy and support are made possible. A brake on optimism about self-help though is that, as in therapy, intimacy might bring abuse as well as care. This triggers my next point.

The emerging literature on minimal interventions
Given the problems of demand exceeding supply of personalised, one-to-one therapy in health care systems, there has been an increasing interest in minimal interventions and self-care, especially in relation to 'common mental health

problems'. This has largely emphasised the prospect of using the minimum input for the maximum mental health gain. The advantage of this prospect is twofold. First, with limited access to therapy the least amount of therapy is cost-effective for health care systems. Second, the less contact patients have with therapists the less they are exposed to iatrogenic deterioration. The latter refers to the adverse impact at times of being in therapy.

To date there is some evidence that a 'stepped care' approach is indeed cost-effective. This involves offering patients with common mental health problems guided self-help or minimal therapy (usually an assessment followed by BIBLIOTHERAPY). The latter entails guiding patients to self-help manuals that are based upon the same principles as CBT. Another version is to offer computerised therapy (cCBT), such as 'Beating the Blues'. Whilst stepped care is effective,[27] there is little evidence that leaving patients on waiting lists with bibliotherapy, without some degree of input or guidance from qualified therapists is effective.[28] This is consistent with the overall findings about psychological treatment mentioned earlier – therapy is more effective than waiting list conditions.

It is also worth recalling at this point that waiting list controls are not static. Patients on waiting lists are not in a form of existential suspended animation. As noted above, when discussing Eysenck's misleading notion of 'spontaneous remission', some patients do get better on waiting lists (and some of course may deteriorate).

One possible scenario of relevance to this question of 'spontaneous remission' is that those who seek out therapy have exhausted sources of help in their everyday networks. In other words, it is possible that help-seeking for mental health problems involves a particular sample of all those with those problems at a moment in time. The latter is called 'point prevalence' and we know from a range of studies of health problems that there is a 'clinical iceberg'.[29] That is, clinical samples do not reflect the total number of people with problems at a moment in time – they are the tip of the iceberg. Moreover, those at the tip who seek help may reflect a personal and social context that is different from those in the rest of the iceberg.

Principled objections to therapy

The above methodological debates within the literature on therapeutic outcomes are only part of the story of that literature. The second form of relevant writing on the topic comes from those who query the very nature of therapy and its legitimacy. Here some examples are noted.

Therapy as a myth

This argument from Szasz[30] was put in Chapter 1 and can be simply accepted or rejected. One either considers that it is useful and acceptable to use medical terminology to describe psychological problems and professional responses to them or one rejects these terms in favour of others (such as 'problems of living', 'presenting problems', 'psychological interventions' or 'counselling' or Szasz's own 'iatrology'). Although this is arguably simply a semantic debate, Szasz does correctly question the logic of turning people with personal troubles and problems of living into patients.

Madness and misery reflect a person's inability to conform to role and rule expectations in their particular society. To turn this inability into a medical condition, and separate it off from our understanding about the rest of human experience and conduct has profound implications. Does it imply that psychological defects are intrinsically and unambiguously inside patients? If so, do we ignore the value judgements used by both lay people and professionals involved in labelling mental health problems (discussed in Chapter 1)? Does it imply that those of us who are not mentally ill are totally responsible for our actions but those of us deemed to be mentally ill are not at all responsible? If the latter group are not responsible, do they also lose their rights to the autonomy of other citizens, who by common consent are mentally 'well'? Does this create two groups of humanity with one being exposed to paternalism at best and at worst to brutal control (shown in the history of psychiatry)?

In my view, the Szaszian objection, which explores these thorny questions, has created a creative climate of debate. For example, some therapists have argued that the social character of madness and misery should encourage us to go beyond medicalisation and seek alternative or additional strategies to therapy.[31] The absolute position taken by Szasz about voluntarism and the myth of psychotherapy prompts these sorts of suggestion. It also prompts us to examine the limits of focusing on individual pathology and brings us to the next point.

Therapy as danger

Some have objected to therapy in principle because they consider it a danger to its clients. The most vociferous example here is that from the ex-psychoanalyst Jeffrey Masson in his *Against Therapy*.[32] From his perspective, therapy is about power and so always leads to abusive outcomes. This rather stark conclusion has some partial evidence base.[33] We certainly know that IATROGENIC DETERIORATION EFFECTS (patients becoming more distressed) are evident in those who suffer abuse at the hands of therapists.[34]

The question is whether Masson's nihilism is warranted. After all, if therapy is effective overall, compared to no treatment, this conclusion absorbs deterioration effects and comes up with a 'balanced score sheet' of positive outcomes (a common picture in many forms of treatment in medicine).

Moreover, this balance suggests that if deterioration effects could be reduced, by reducing incompetence and abuse in therapy, then the outcome would be even more impressive.

Nonetheless, Masson's objection has drawn attention to denial and complacency in many in the therapy industry about abuse. Anonymous surveys of therapists from a variety of professional backgrounds in Britain and North America have found that between 0.8% and 7% of therapists report sexual contact with their clients. Some of these reported serial abuse.[35]

Thus abusive therapists are in the minority but client complaints about abuse and its consequences might radically undermine the reputation of talking treatments. If the placebo effect is important in these treatments then public confidence is an important matter. Also, the evidence about abuse punctures some cultural myths about talking treatments always being a benign alternative to biological treatments. The aphorism that 'it's good to talk' is certainly a questionable cliché; in some contexts undoubtedly 'talking only makes it worse'.

Therapy as a diversion: The need for more love and social change

At the same time that Masson's attack emerged from North American psychoanalysis, the British clinical psychologist David Smail launched his own critique of therapy. This focused less on its iatrogenic risks than its diversionary nature. In *Taking Care: An Alternative to Therapy,* Smail argues that therapists should think less about changing people and more about what they learn about how people change. Moreover, the empiricist desire, to develop mechanistic rationales or laws about change, fails to do justice to the existential complexity of patients and their lives.[36]

A second point Smail makes relates to the flaw in 'looking on the bright side of life' encouraged by cognitive therapy. He argues instead that reality *really is* corrosive of mental health and that patients have not inevitably 'got it wrong' in their view of their miserable world.

Smail's third main point is that if there is a genuine healing component in therapy it comes from the therapist's love. And, he goes on, love is an ordinary human quality – it is not derived from all the training, credentials and clever rationales bound up with the therapy industry. He argues, therefore, that what we need is not technologies of change (the therapies) but social relationships which are dominated by care for others (hence the quotation I cite at the start of this chapter). Smail's logic about the limitations of therapy is elaborated further in his subsequent book *How to Survive without Psychotherapy*.[37]

Therapy according to social science

Apart from the above debates within the mental health industry about the effectiveness or worth of therapy, the latter has attracted considerable interest from social scientists. I mention these commentaries here not so much because they contain some criticisms of therapy (which they do implicitly or explicitly) but because they situate psychological treatment in a socio-historical context.

The 'civilising process' evident in modern societies brought with it the importance of self-consciousness about manners and etiquette.[38] With this came self-regulation not just state-imposed social control. Most of us in developed societies know when we are violating 'emotion rules'.[39] This ability of modern citizens self-consciously to understand emotional normality and abnormality has come with a stress on the importance of managing our emotional expression in social transactions, including as employees.[40]

This taken-for-granted skill then leads to two groups of potential patients (as I noted in Chapter 1). There are those of us who, *because* we identify our emotional rule-breaking (i.e. we feel miserable), seek help. However, there are others of us who become patients because we *do not* recognise our emotional rule-breaking. Others though are offended, perplexed or frightened by the deviant person's conduct. Psychotic patients or others who are 'lacking in insight', such as those with a diagnosis of Asperger's syndrome, or obsessive-compulsive personality disorder or histrionic personality disorder, are created in this social process.

The rise of therapeutic interventions to deal with emotional rule-breaking in advanced capitalist societies in the twentieth century displaced religious frames of reference. Foucault makes the point that therapy is the secular legacy of the confessional:

> The confession has spread its effects far and wide. It plays a part in justice, medicine, education, family relationships, in love relations, in the most ordinary affairs of everyday life and in the most solemn rites; one confesses one's crimes, one's sins, one's thoughts and desires, one's illnesses and troubles; one goes about telling with the greatest precision whatever it is most difficult to tell.[41]

Therapy and the culture of narcissism
Democratic secularism could offer therapeutic rationales that could explore the meaning of life for the non-religious and promote the autonomy of those individuals detrimentally affected by anxiety, sadness, guilt, alienation and any other neurotic symptom generated by the legacy of childhood or the current pressures of modern life. Within these accounts, emotional life is explored and challenged in order to promote individual freedom and improve well-being.

What the authors disagree about is whether this process of secular individualism (what Christopher Lasch calls a 'culture of narcissism') is benign or manipulative. For example, Abram de Swaan, a Dutch sociologist interested in the 'management of normality' in modern societies is of the opinion that therapy is an ambiguous form of social control but suggests that on balance we are better with it than without it. (See his quotation at the start of this chapter.) By contrast, Frank Furedi, a British sociologist, is more suspicious and concludes that:

> Therapy, like the wider culture of which it is a part, teaches people to know their place. In return it offers the dubious blessings of affirmation and recognition.[42]

The prestigious British economist, Richard Layard, has recently entered this debate about the socio-economic worth of therapy.[43] He argues that it is cost-effective to supply therapy because mild to moderate mental health problems are a removable fiscal burden on the state. He believes that therapy is a technical fix for this burden – it can get people out of health care and welfare dependency and into work. At the same time, he is critical of modern societal values, which focus on greedy individualism, and he notes that as we have become richer we are not any happier. This is because we are trapped on the 'Hedonic Treadmill', believing falsely that the next consumed product will deliver happiness. Of course it does not, because one is waiting in the wings with another false promise.

In line with Foucault's earlier point about the confessional mode of modern life, Rose talks of 'the psychologization of the mundane', 'a therapeutic of finitude' and a 'neurotization of social intercourse'.[44] Unlike Furedi, who depicts therapy as a process of political mystification (for example, poverty he argues is now framed as a mental health problem) and a way of cultivating conformity, Rose is neutral about its political role. His view, with that of his collaborator Peter Miller, is made very clear here in this discussion of mental health work in regulatory systems of the state:

> We argue that it is more fruitful to consider the ways that
> regulatory systems have sought to promote subjectivity than
> to document the ways in which they have crushed it.[45]

This quotation highlights that, as with professional researchers in the field and client accounts of therapy, our recent dominant notion of psychological treatment is in the voluntary, particularly individual, mode. However, as I have noted earlier, psychological treatment has now been applied increasingly in coercive contexts. The latter were previously stereotyped as arenas of impersonal, dehumanising forms of biological treatment. But psychological treatment has encroached increasingly into community mental health teams with a strong surveillance brief, secure hospitals and prisons with their large quota of mentally disordered offenders.

Manifestations of the modern obsession with the self are certainly all around us, with vanity plates on cars and funerals favouring the refrains of 'My Way' or 'I Will Survive'. The regular middle-aged train passenger encounters teenagers preoccupied with their text messages and personalised ring tones, seemingly enjoyed with a crass indifference to those around them. Hair products must be bought 'Because you're worth it' and cars are sold to 'Search for the hero inside of you!' Musical download advertisements for mobile phones can offer the new customer the 'soundtrack of your life'. This commodification of the boastful, hungry and flattered ego both shapes and responds to the particular self-centredness of the 'Me Generation' raised by the rules of neo-liberal capitalism. However, those of all ages are caught up in its web – the culture of personal entitlement now infects us all. Getting what we want has become a human right – because we're worth it.

The current preoccupation with celebrity and the desire to be famous as a goal in itself, rather than it being a by-product of proven talent or genuine social merit, are other examples of the norm of narcissism in modern culture. The seemingly unending hunger for 'reality TV', which turns unremarkable people into ephemeral heroes and villains, may suggest that Andy Warhol was right – 'everybody will be world-famous for fifteen minutes'. Maybe personal therapy can just be added to this long cultural roll call of egotism and the modern obsession with individual choice and public display as the touchstone of the good life. However, this real-enough catalogue of modern self-centredness tends only to reflect superficial self-regard and vanity, whereas pain, insecurity and despair are typically the focus of therapy. I genuinely think that for most therapists and clients it is not an ego trip. Nonetheless, the possible link between therapy and vanity does bear examination, especially if it is offered as simply another consumer product to fix problems for egotistical individuals, without reference to their social context.

Individualism and individual therapy

The above-summarised sociological commentaries are overwhelmingly preoccupied with individual therapy for existential woes and 'mild to moderate mental health problems'. The debates centre on the value we should place on 'technologies of the self' (help or hindrance? mystifying or demystifying? exploring our individuality or putting us in our place?). What they agree on though is that the therapy culture is an example of what Foucault called 'productive power' in society – it produces selves or the view people have of themselves. Therapeutic talk inscribes onto clients a version of being a person.

This debate does not address though the spectrum of coercion I introduced in Chapter 2. In particular the authors do not examine the application of psychological treatment at the harsher end of the spectrum of coercion. In this case there is no ambiguity about whether therapy is a form of repressive control, rather than a method to construct and affirm the autonomous individual and their self-referential preoccupations. When coercion is evident then psychological treatment becomes part of the repressive wing of the State. The only point at issue is whether within involuntary settings it is preferable to use drugs or talk to achieve the desired end. Is it more acceptable to involuntary and pseudo-voluntary clients and is it more effective in the eyes of those who pay for and run the mental health system than biological interventions and containment?

Conclusions and loose ends

In the earlier chapters I outlined the overall logic or rationale for psychological treatment and described the parties involved. In the previous chapter I looked at the trustworthiness of therapy. In this chapter, following from that, I have dwelt on the 'is it worth it?' question. Each reader will draw their own conclusions about this from their own experience and from the sorts of costs and benefits that can be weighed up, given the list of considerations I provide above. In this final section of the book I want to offer the following personal reflections.

The strong case for the placebo model
Psychological treatment may merit our personal and public policy investment but I am less convinced that the professionally preferred rationales for personal change are persuasive. Put differently, each rationale is sort of persuasive (provided that you engage with it credulously) but if they are all so different and yet persuasive, why be particularly convinced by any one? The fact that there are so many competing claims makes any one suspect. It also makes one suspect the special pleading of any particular claim.

The comparison between types of psychological treatment and religious sects is fairly evident in modern society, as I noted in Chapter 2. And if treatment outperforms waiting lists but does not outperform placebo wings in trials, could it simply be that any rationale will be helpful, provided that it features benign consistency, consideration and confidence from the therapist and the client is open to change? As I noted in Chapter 2 this is not to belittle the role of placebo. The latter is useful both to provide and to explore and conceptualise – it is not a trivial matter because it points to the role of interpersonal faith or non-erotic love and its power to enable personal change. In order for the therapist to have confidence in their contribution to that change, they must believe in the model they deploy and apply it consistently: hence the paradox of treatment fidelity noted above.

Pluralism is guaranteed

The state of psychological treatment reflects the state of human science. Unless this is noted with care, those new to the field might believe that the therapy industry is highly variegated because it is simply a weird or quirky marketplace of products. In fact, all efforts at human science in the overlapping disciplines of philosophy, psychology, anthropology, history, political science, human geography, economics and sociology predictably end up with competing theories and knowledge claims.

Foucault makes the point that by the beginning of the nineteenth century three planes of inquiry began to constitute knowledge or the modern 'episteme'. These were first the sciences of maths and physics, which could work things out in advance. Second, there were the sciences, like biology and geography, which described and explained things after careful observation. Third, there was philosophical reflection.[46]

Foucault argued that the human sciences operate in the fluid spaces *between* these three planes of knowledge.[47] As a consequence, the human sciences are free legitimately to explore a wide range of theories and methods. They consequently end up generating many different models about human action and experience. Arguments inevitably then abound about methods to be used (qualitative or quantitative), scientifically legitimate content (experience or behaviour) and levels of analysis (body, mind, social system).

However there is an inconsistent relationship between human science and psychological treatment. If we start with the three main links between human science and treatment (ASSOCIATIONISM; PSYCHOANALYSIS; and EXISTENTIALISM) there is an uneven reciprocal relationship. PSYCHOANALYSIS is the only one of the three that started in the clinic and expanded to become a distinct form of psychological knowledge. There was a constant interplay thereafter between clinical and theoretical concerns.

This is not the case with the other two. It is noteworthy that ASSOCIATIONISM (described in Chapter 2, with its two offsprings of BEHAVIOURISM and COGNITIVISM) by and large developed separately from therapy. Certainly some behaviourists (like Skinner and Pavlov) advocated the use of psychological knowledge to explain and treat neurosis. The case with cognitivism is less convincing though – most of the therapeutic innovations in COGNITIVE THERAPY were made by practical clinicians. For example, Ellis and Beck were not immersed in the cognitive science emerging in the discipline of general psychology, subsequently, during the 1970s, to displace behaviourism as the dominant academic model. Both were disillusioned by psychoanalysis, with its neutrality about goals and its austere curiosity about irrationality, and they favoured more direct ways to challenge negative or irrational views held by patients. They did theorise and they were influenced by ancient philosophy but their innovations were *not* from contemporary cognitive science in psychology.

When we turn to EXISTENTIALISM, this philosophy was developed independently of therapy but its main interest (the study of existence and its personal implications for reflective beings living finite lives) is inherently close to the sort of conversation that happens in most forms of therapy. Indeed it can be argued that all forms of therapy are to an extent concerned with existential matters because they entail therapists attending credulously to a story a person tells about their life. It is impossible to be interested in biography without it being at some level an existential exploration.

The role of therapy in modern society is ambiguous

I mentioned that sociological commentators on therapy vary in their judgement about its benign, oppressive or mystifying role. It can be framed in different ways. For health planners and some psychiatrists, psychological treatment is simply one mode within a 'therapeutic armamentarium' (the complete range of available methods of treatment). This medical framework has been criticised by many but it retains a strong legitimacy. For many radical critics from within the mental health professions therapy is a clear humane alternative to biological psychiatry.

The problem with this argument (which in younger days I supported and promoted) is that it assumes that therapeutic relationships are inevitably benign – that it is always 'good to talk'. We now know that this idealisation of talk is unfounded. Therapists can and do, in various ways, exploit their clients and this often leads to deterioration, rather than an improvement, in mental health. This danger culminates in critics pointing out that therapy should be avoided in the interest of mental health and that true autonomy is diminished not enhanced by therapy.

So, returning to the question in this chapter's heading, is psychological treatment worth the investment? In the light of the above discussion the answer is ambiguous – or more precisely it depends on who is asking the question and why. For example, if Furedi is correct in his analysis, then vulnerability and dependency are encouraged in individuals as a means of obscuring their social and economic relations and keeping people in their place in society. This implies a gain for those who benefit from the retention of the socio-economic status quo.

If Rose is correct, then therapy, along with many other processes in modern societies, has psychologised our social existence. To use de Swaan's phrase, more and more of us have been 'proto-professionalised' to think in therapeutic terms, whether or not we are actually in therapy. But this reflects productive power – modern identities are produced not crushed by these processes. Rose thus has a much more benign (or neutral) view of the therapy industry than Furedi.

The empirical evidence is that these sociological generalisations and conclusions may reflect partial trends but they are flawed because they assume that psychological treatment has no coercive role (i.e. that is only a 'soft' form of social regulation or 'productive power'). However, it is clear now that psychological treatment does play a role in coercive settings. As a consequence, different communities of interest in the four domains I noted in the introduction to this chapter would certainly address the core question about investment in different ways.

Politicians and civil servants will want to know what works in order to justify investment from the public purse. Both the suppliers and recipients of voluntary existential exploration would consider therapy a good investment and so together will promote and maintain a private sector of treatment. The client in primary care who does not want pills for their distress might prefer talking treatment.

But, as we shift down the coercive continuum, the goals of therapy shift from existential clarification and the reduction of symptoms of distress to ones about risk to self and others. As a consequence, criteria of success are now different. The main point is whether therapy is effective at reducing risk. Does therapy increase the chances that the recipient will act in a less risky way? If risk is reduced there may be secondary benefits to them of personal growth and liberty but the starting point is not these goals but others about risk reduction, set by third parties.

Of course the paedophile prisoner with no real desire to alter his sexual proclivities will refuse the offer of therapy or comply disingenuously with the demand. As for the psychotic voice hearer, detained forcibly in hospital, should he or she be cured with therapy or liberated with tolerance? It is not self-evident that being mad is an undesirable state, although the dominant current view is that this is the case. This is why even those who have moved to a psychological model and away from assumptions about biological causes and treatments, debate whether we should let madness be or seek to alter its manifestations using therapy.[48] The emphasis of Szasz on voluntarism still preoccupies us.[49] Should therapy only be about respecting the voluntary contact, and increasing the autonomy of the client? Even sociological commentators have mixed views about this. This loose end to the book is left for us all to ponder.

Endnotes

Chapter 1

1. Masson, JM (1989) *Against Therapy: Warning – Psychotherapy may be hazardous to your mental health.* London: Harper Collins.

2. Szasz, TS (1979) *The Myth of Psychotherapy*. New York: Anchor Press.

3. Boyle, M (1999) Diagnosis. In C Newnes, G Holmes & C Dunn (eds) *This Is Madness: A critical look at psychiatry and the future of mental health services.* Ross-on-Wye: PCCS Books.

4. American Psychiatric Association (1994) *Diagnostic and Statistical Manual of Mental Disorders* (4th ed). Washington DC: APA

5. World Health Organization (1992) *The ICD-10 Classification of Mental and Behavioural Disorders.* Geneva: WHO.

6. Coulter, J (1973) *Approaches to Insanity.* London: Martin Robertson.

7. Lord Reid, cited in Jones, R (1991) *Mental Health Act Manual* (3rd ed). London: Sweet and Maxwell.

8. Hoggett, B (1990) *Mental Health Law.* London: Sweet and Maxwell.

9. Pilgrim, D (2007) The survival of psychiatric diagnosis. *Social Science and Medicine, 65* (3), 536–44.

10. National Alliance for the Mentally Ill (2002) *Understanding Major Depression. What you need to know about this medical illness.* Arlinton VA: National Alliance for the Mentally Ill.

11. Oxman, RB (2005) *A Fractured Mind: My life with multiple personality disorder.* New York: Hyperion.

12. Department of Health (2004) *Draft Mental Health Bill (2: 5).* London: Department of Health.

13. Pilgrim, D (2005) *Key Concepts in Mental Health*. London: Sage.

14. Pilgrim, D (2002) The biopsychosocial model in Anglo-American psychiatry: Past, present and future? *Journal of Mental Health 11*(6), 585–94; and Double, D (1990) What would Adolf Meyer have thought about the neo-Kraepelinian approach? *Psychiatric Bulletin 1*, 471–4.

15. Levenson, H (1995) *Time-Limited Dynamic Psychotherapy*. New York: Basic Books.

Chapter 2

1. Laing, RD (1970) *The Politics of Experience and the Bird of Paradise*. Harmondsworth: Penguin.

2. Feltham, C (2006) Types of goal. In C Feltham & I Horton (eds) (2006) *The Sage Handbook of Counselling and Psychotherapy.* London: Sage.

3. Rogers, CR (1957) The necessary and sufficient conditions of therapeutic personality change. *Journal of Consulting Psychology 21*, 95–103.

4. Feltham, C (ed) (1997) *Which Psychotherapy? Leading exponents explain their differences*. London: Sage.

5. Pentony, P (1981) *Models of Influence in Psychotherapy*. New York: Free Press.

6. See Frank, JD (1973) *Persuasion and Healing: A comparative study of psychotherapy*. Baltimore, MD: John Hopkins Press; Gillis, JS (1979) *Social Influence in Psychotherapy*. Jonesboro, TN: Pilgrimage Press; Torrey, EF see n. 8.

7. Fish, JM (1973) *Placebo Therapy*. San Francisco CA: Jossey-Bass.

8. Torrey, EF (1972) What Western psychotherapists can learn from witchdoctors. *American Journal of Orthopsychiatry 42*, 69–76.

9. Watts, A (1970) *Psychotherapy East and West*. Harmondsworth: Penguin.

10. Truax, CB & Mitchell, KM (1971) Research into certain therapist interpersonal skills in relation to process and outcome. In AE Bergin & SL Garfield (eds) *Handbook of Psychotherapy and Behavior Change.* New York: Wiley.

11. Yates, A (1975) *Behaviour Therapy*. London: Wiley.

12. Schein, EH (1973) Personal change through interpersonal relationships. In WG Bennis et al (eds) *Interpersonal Dynamics: Essays and readings in human interaction.* Homewood, IL: Dorsey.

13. See Bateson, G (1972) *Steps to an Ecology of Mind*. New York: Ballantine; Watzlawick, P, Weakland, JH & Fisch, R (1974) *Change: Principles of problem formation and problem resolution*. New York: Norton; and Haley, J (1976) *Problem Solving Therapy: New strategies of effective family therapy*. New York: Harper and Row.

14. Page 69 in Lax, WD (1992) Postmodern thinking in clinical practice. In S McNamee & KJ Gergen (eds) *Therapy as Social Construction.* London: Sage.

15. Dryden, W (ed) (2002) *Handbook of Individual Therapy*. London: Sage.

Endnotes pp. 16–26

16. Pines, M & Schlapobersky, J (2000) Group methods in adult psychiatry. In MG Gelder, JJ Lopez-Ibor & NC Andreasen (eds) *The New Oxford Textbook of Psychiatry.* Oxford: Oxford University Press.

17. Yalom, I (1985) *Existential Psychotherapy.* New York: Basic Books.

18. Feltham, C & Horton, I (eds) (2006) *The Sage Handbook of Counselling and Psychotherapy.* London: Sage.

19. Kelly, G (1955) *The Psychology of Personal Constructs.* New York: Norton.

20. Woolfe, R, Dryden, W & Strawbridge, S (2003) *Handbook of Counselling Psychology.* London: Sage.

21. See Knight, L (1986) *Talking to a Stranger: A consumer's guide to therapy.* London: Fontana; France, A (1988) *Consuming Psychotherapy.* London: Free Associations Books; and Sands, A (2000) *Falling for Therapy: Psychotherapy from a client's point of view.* London: Macmillan.

22. Feltham, C (ed) (1997) *Which Psychotherapy? Leading exponents explain their differences.* London: Sage.

23. Morris, B (2005) *Discovering Bits and Pieces of Me: Research exploring women's experience of psychoanalytical therapy.* London: Women's Therapy Centre.

24. Bion, WR (1961) *Experiences in Groups.* London: Tavistock.

25. See Bion, ibid; and Foulkes, SH (1964) *Therapeutic Group Analysis.* London: International Universities Press.

26. Carpenter, J & Treacher, A (1989) *Problems and Solutions in Marital and Family Therapy.* Oxford: Blackwell.

27. Bateson, G (1972) *Steps to an Ecology of Mind.* New York: Ballantine.

28. Feltham, C & Horton, I (eds) (2006) *The Sage Handbook of Counselling and Psychotherapy.* London: Sage.

29. Palmer, S & McMahon, G (eds) (1997) *Handbook of Counselling.* London: Routledge.

30. Rees, TP (1957) Back to moral treatment and community care. *Journal of Mental Science 103*, 303.

31. Campling, P & Haigh, R (eds) (1999) *Therapeutic Communities: Past, present and future.* London: Jessica Kingsley.

32. Cooper, D (1968) *Psychiatry and Anti-Psychiatry.* London: Tavistock.

33. Pedriali, E (1997) Italian therapeutic communities: From historical analysis to hypothesis for change. *Therapeutic Communities 18*(4), 285–96.

34. Woodward, R (1999) The prison communities: Therapy within a custodial setting. In P Campling & R Haigh (eds) *Therapeutic Communities: Past, present and future.* London: Jessica Kingsley.

35. Welldon, EV & Van Velsen, C (eds) (1997*) A Practical Guide to Forensic Psychotherapy.* London: Jessica Kingsley.

36. Ibid; and van Marle, H (1997) *Challenges in Forensic Psychotherapy.* London: Jessica Kingsley.

37. Hollin, CR (1995) The meaning and implications of 'Programme Integrity'. In J McGuire (ed) *What Works? Reducing reoffending.* London: Wiley.

38. Prentky, R (1995) A rationale for the treatment of sex offenders. In J McGuire (ed) *What Works? Reducing reoffending.* London: Wiley.

39. Dryden, W (ed) (2002) *Handbook of Individual Therapy.* London: Sage.

Chapter 3

1. Sutherland, S (1998) *Breakdown.* London: Weidenfeld & Nicolson.

2. Morris, B (2005) *Discovering Bits and Pieces of Me: Research exploring women's experience of psychoanalytical therapy.* London: Women's Therapy Centre; and Faulkner, A & Layzell, S (2000) *Strategies for Living: A report of user-led research into people's strategies for living with mental distress.* London: The Mental Health Foundation.

3. Szasz, TS (1963) The concept of transference. *International Journal of Psycho-Analysis 44,* 432–43.

4. Langs, R (1990) *Psychotherapy: A basic text.* Northvale NJ: Jason Aronson.

5. Masson, JM (1984) *The Assault on Truth: Freud's suppression of the seduction theory.* London: Faber and Faber.

6. Masson, JM (1989) *Against Therapy: Warning – Psychotherapy may be hazardous to your mental health.* London: HarperCollins.

7. Stone, J (2002) Evaluating the ethical and legal content of professional codes. In J Allsop & M Saks (eds) *Regulating the Health Professions.* London: Sage.

8. Price, D (2002) Legal aspects of the regulation of the health professions. In J Allsop & M Saks (eds) *Regulating the Health Professions.* London: Sage.

9. Strasburger, LH, Jorgenson, L & Randles, R (1996) Criminalization of psychotherapist-patient sex. In DN Bersoff (ed) *Ethical Conflicts in Psychology.* Washington DC: American Psychological Association.

10. Larson, MS (1977) *The Rise of Professionalism: A sociological analysis.* Berkeley CA: University of California Press.

Endnotes pp. 38–52

11. Johnson, T (1995) Governmentality and the institutionalisation of expertise. In T Johnson, G Larkin & M Saks (eds) *Health Professions and the State in Europe*. London: Routledge.

12. The Statement can be accessed here: http://ipnosis.postle.net/SRStatementOpposition.htm

13. Allsop, J (2002) Regulation and the medical profession. In J Allsop & M Saks (eds) *Regulating the Health Professions*. London: Sage.

14. Stacey, M (1992) *Regulating British Medicine: The General Medical Council*. Chichester: Wiley.

15. Price, D (2002) Legal aspects of the regulation of the health professions. In J Allsop & M Saks (eds) *Regulating the Health Professions*. London: Sage.

16. This position is suggested by Masson JM (1989) *Against Therapy: Warning – Psychotherapy may be hazardous to your mental health*. London: HarperCollins.

17. Davies, C (1999) Rethinking regulation in the health professions in the UK: Institutions, ideals and identities. In I Hellberg, M Saks & C Benoit (eds) *Professional Identities in Transition*. Sodertalje: Almqvist and Wiksell International; and Davies, C (2000) *Professional Self-Regulation: Is there an alternative?* Stakeholder Regulation: A discussion paper. London: Royal College of Nursing.

Chapter 4

1. See page 1, Smail, D (1987) *Taking Care: An alternative to therapy*. London: Constable.

2. See page 16, Swaan, A de (1990) *The Management of Normality*. London: Routledge.

3. Donabedian, A (1992) The role of outcomes in quality assessment and assurance. *Quality Review Bulletin 18*, 356–60.

4. Tolley, K & Rowland, N (1995) *Evaluating the Cost-Effectiveness of Counselling in Health Care.* London: Routledge.

5. Barkham, M (2007) Methods, outcomes and processes in the psychological therapies across four successive research generations. In W Dryden (ed) *Dryden's Handbook of Individual Therapy.* London: Sage; and Bower, P & Barkham, M (2006) Evidence-based practice in counselling and psychotherapy: Definition, philosophy and critique. In C Feltham & I Horton (eds) *The Sage Handbook of Counselling and Psychotherapy.* London: Sage.

6. Yates, A (1975) *Behaviour Therapy*. London: Wiley.

7. Department of Health (2001) *Treatment Choice in Psychological Therapies and Counselling: Evidence-based clinical practice guidelines*. London: Department of Health.

8. Barkham, M (2007) Methods, outcomes and processes in the psychological therapies across four successive research generations. In W Dryden (ed) *Dryden's Handbook of Individual Therapy*. London: Sage.

9. Page 111 in Paul, G (1967) Strategy in outcome research in psychotherapy. *Journal of Consulting Psychology 31*, 109–18.

10. Seligman, MEP (1995) The effectiveness of psychotherapy: The Consumer Reports study. *American Psychologist 50*, 965–74.

11. Department of Health (2001) *Treatment Choice in Psychological Therapies and Counselling: Evidence-based clinical practice guidelines*. London: Department of Health; and Layard, R (2005) *Happiness*. London: Penguin.

12. Prentky, R (1995) A rationale for the treatment of sex offenders. In J McGuire (ed) *What Works? Reducing reoffending*. London: Wiley.

13. Bower, P & Barkham, M (2006) Evidence-based practice in counselling and psychotherapy: Definition, philosophy and critique. In C Feltham & I Horton (eds) *The Sage Handbook of Counselling and Psychotherapy*. London: Sage.

14. Erwin, E (1997) *Philosophy and Psychotherapy*. London: Sage.

15. McLeod, J (2006) Research and evaluation in counselling. In C Feltham & I Horton (eds) *The Sage Handbook of Counselling and Psychotherapy*. London: Sage.

16. Page 161 in Erwin, E (1997) *Philosophy and Psychotherapy*. London: Sage

17. Rogers, CR (1955) Persons or science? A philosophical question. *American Psychologist 10*, 267–78.

18. Smail, D (1987) *Taking Care: An alternative to therapy*. London: Constable.

19. Seligman, MEP (1995) The effectiveness of psychotherapy: The Consumer Reports study. *American Psychologist 50*, 965–74.

20. Brown, T & Harris, G (1978) *Social Origins of Depression*. London: Tavistock.

21. Pilgrim, D & Bentall, RP (1999) The medicalisation of misery: A critical realist analysis of the concept of depression. *Journal of Mental Health 8* (3), 261–74.

22. Murray, CJL & Lopez, AD (eds) (1995) *The Global Burden of Disease*. Cambridge MA: Harvard University Press.

23. Fernando, S (1991) *Mental Health, Race and Culture*. Basingstoke: Macmillan.

24. Lambert, M, Ogles, BM & Masters, KS (1992) Choosing outcome assessment devices: An organisational and conceptual scheme. *Journal of Counseling and Development 70*, 527–32.

25. Stratton, P (2005) *Report on the evidence base of systemic family therapy*. Warrington: Association of Family Therapy.

26. Eysenck, HJ (1952) The effects of psychotherapy: An evaluation. *Journal of Consulting Psychology 16*, 319–24.

27. Richards, A, Barkham, M, Cahill, J, Richards, D, Williams, C & Heywood, P (2003) PHASE: A randomised controlled trial of supervised self-help and cognitive behaviour therapy in primary care. *British Journal of General Practice 53*, 764–70.

28. Mead, N, MacDonald, W, Bower, P, Lovell, K, Richards, D, Roberts, C & Bucknall, A (2005) The clinical effectiveness of guided self-help versus waiting list control in the management of anxiety and depression: A randomised controlled trial. *Psychological Medicine 35*, 1633–43.

29. Hannay, D (1979) *The Symptom Iceberg: A study of community health*. London: Routledge.

30. Szasz, TS (1979) *The Myth of Psychotherapy*. New York: Anchor Press.

31. Dowrick, C (2004) *Beyond Depression: A new approach to understanding and management*. Oxford: Oxford University Press; and Smail, D (1996) *Getting By Without Psychotherapy*. London: Constable.

32. Masson, JM (1989) *Against Therapy: Warning – Psychotherapy may be hazardous to your mental health*. London: HarperCollins.

33. Pilgrim, D & Guinan, P (1999) From mitigation to culpability: Rethinking the evidence about therapist sexual abuse. *European Journal of Counselling, Psychotherapy and Health 2*(2), 153–68.

34. Pope, KS & Bouhoutsos, JC (1986) *Sexual Intimacy between Therapists and Patients*. New York: Praeger; and Benowitz, M (1995) Comparing the experiences of women clients sexually exploited by female versus male psychotherapists. In JC Gonssiorek (ed) *Breach of Trust: Sexual exploitation by health care professionals and clergy*. London: Sage.

35. Szymanska, K & Palmer, S (1997) Counsellor-client exploitation. In S Palmer & G McMahon (eds) *Handbook of Counselling*. London: Routledge.

36. Smail, D (1987) *Taking Care: An alternative to therapy*. London: Constable.

37. Smail, D (1996) *How to Survive without Psychotherapy*. London: Constable.

38. Elias, N (1978) *The Civilising Process*. Oxford: Blackwell.

39. Thoits, PA (1985) Self-labeling processes in mental illness: The role of emotional deviance. *American Journal of Sociology 91*, 221–49; and Rose, N (1990) *Governing the Soul: The shaping of the private self*. London: Routledge.

40. Hochschild, A (1983) *The Managed Heart: Commercialization of human feeling*. Berkeley CA: University of California Press.

41. Page 59 in Foucault, M (1981) *The History of Sexuality, Vol 1, trans. Robert Hurley*. New York: Vintage Books.

42. Page 204 in Furedi, F (2004) *Therapy Culture: Cultivating uncertainty in an uncertain age*. London: Routledge.

43. Layard, R (2005) *Happiness*. London: Penguin.

44. Rose, N (1990) *Governing the Soul: The shaping of the private self*. London: Routledge.

45. Miller, P & Rose, N (1988) The Tavistock programme: The government of subjectivity and social life. *Sociology 22*(2), 171–92.

46. Foucault, M (1973) *The Order of Things: An archaeology of the human sciences*. New York: Vintage Books.

47. Smart, B (1990) On the disorder of things: Sociology and the end of the social. *Sociology 29*, 397–416.

48. Bentall, R (2003) *Madness Explained: Psychosis and Human Nature* London: Penguin; May, R (2000) Routes to recovery from psychosis: The roots of a clinical psychologist. *Clinical Psychology Forum 146*, 6–10.

49. Szasz, TS (1979) *The Myth of Psychotherapy*. New York: Anchor Press.

Glossary

This glossary provides the reader with short explanatory commentaries about those words in the text that point to complex topics in their own right. Most of the entries provide one or two references for further reading (see pp. 120–2).

ALIENATION in current usage indicates patients' feeling of distance or separation from themselves or from others. EXISTENTIAL thinking sees a cause of alienation as due to conformity to society, with a loss of connection to a person's 'real self'. There was a lay view, prior to the twentieth century, that madness is under the alien influence of the moon (hence 'lunacy'). Specifically, 'alienists' were medical men in the early nineteenth century who looked after lunatics, a connotation that was derived from the Latin *alienare* meaning to 'deprive of reason'. This emphasis on reason indicates a shift from an earlier period in antiquity when the non-rational was valued, to it being devalued and held in constant suspicion. For example, Socrates considered that madness and sanity had equal value. With the emergence of modernity, rationality became a crucial personal attribute for all citizens to ensure moral order and economic efficiency. Those who lacked or had lost their reason due to idiocy or insanity threatened that order and efficiency. A number of psychotherapists influenced by the Marxian notion of alienation under capitalism, such as David Cooper and Erich Fromm, suggested that insanity and normality are equidistant from true sanity. (Screech, 1985; Leuder & Thomas, 2000)

ASSOCIATIONISM developed as the basis for modern academic psychology in the nineteenth century, from British EMPIRICISM. Philosophers in this school (Locke, Berkley and Hume) argued that there were no innate aspects to experience and behaviour. Instead humans encounter experiences through their senses and these affect what is remembered to guide future action. Associations are thus built up, as the child develops, between action and experience and between inner events themselves (thoughts and feelings). Associationism is the forerunner in modern psychology of both BEHAVIOURISM and COGNITIVISM. Even in those forms of therapy which are outside these two traditions, learned associations of various sorts are recurrently seen as important. In other words, many forms of therapy place learning, especially from childhood, at the centre of their theories. This singular emphasis on learning (with the mind as a blank sheet at birth) has been challenged by many though, including some psychoanalysts who have emphasised innate experiences and impulses, present at birth (e.g. Melanie Klein) and some philosophers of language (Noam Chomsky). (Hearnshaw, 1987; Murphy, 1964)

ATTACHMENT THEORY was developed by the British psychoanalyst John Bowlby who incorporated the implications of studies of early infant–parent attachments in animal studies. This led him to study attachment and loss in young children. He traced feelings of depression and anxiety to these early developmental difficulties. (King, 2006)

BEHAVIOUR THERAPY describes any form of therapy which is derived from BEHAVIOURISM. In particular it applies the conditioned reflexes demonstrated by Ivan Pavlov and his followers as well as operant conditioning (the reinforcement of particular actions studied by Skinner and his followers) to mental health problems. The term 'behaviour modification' tends more narrowly to be applied to the use of operant conditioning. By contrast, behaviour therapists largely focus on undoing conditioned reflexes (especially conditioned fear). Behaviour therapy and modification are based largely on positive and negative reinforcement. Punishment is rarely used. (Marks, 1987; Lovell, 2006)

BEHAVIOURISM is both a method in academic psychology and a philosophy of science. The methodological emphasis is on collecting behavioural data to build up a body of psychological knowledge. The philosophical emphasis is on defining science strictly by the study of outward behaviour – thus the study of thoughts and feelings, as subjective reports, is deemed by behaviourists to be unscientific. Both methodological and philosophical behaviourism emphasise learnt behaviour. In modern psychology two main types of learned behaviour are of interest. The first, studied by Ivan Pavlov and other Russian 'reflexologists' at the turn of the twentieth century, is called 'classical conditioning' (where the reflexes are conditioned by particular stimuli). The second, studied and promoted later, most notably by the American psychologist Burrhus Skinner, is where an action (an operant) increases in probability because of a reinforcing stimulus being present (called 'positive reinforcement' or in lay terms a 'reward') or decreases in probability because it is not reinforced (the response is ignored, technically called 'negative reinforcement'). If the response is met with an aversive stimulus (it is punished) then it may also reduce in probability but this is less efficient than negative reinforcement and might even lead to alternative 'maladaptive' responses. The latter refer to new problems defined by the behaviourist. Because of the emphasis on the relationship between a stimulus and a behavioural response, behaviourism is sometimes called 'S-R' psychology.

BIBLIOTHERAPY describes the use of books and articles to help people with mental health problems. The development of information technology has extended this tradition into the present, including the use of interactive, computer-based therapy. Sometimes therapists use the term in a disparaging way to highlight the importance of true therapy. However, others use it more positively. For example, in minimal interventions and stepped care, self-help texts may be recommended to clients or even given to them as part of the helping relationship. Bibliotherapy has been associated historically with popular psychology and its self-help texts. Today in bookshops these books, intended for a lay audience, can be found alongside academic and clinical texts from and for the helping professions. (Cheshire & Pilgrim, 2004)

COGNITIVE ANALYTICAL THERAPY (CAT) was developed by the British general practitioner, Anthony Ryle during the 1980s. He integrated PERSONAL CONSTRUCT THERAPY and PSYCHOANALYSIS into a style of therapy that is highly collaborative and entails the client mapping repeated patterns of difficulty in their lives. Ryle summarised these recurring problems as 'traps', 'dilemmas' and 'snags'. Traps are negative assumptions that create self-fulfilling prophecies. Dilemmas involve the patient only seeing two contrasting options ('false dichotomies') rather than a range of possibilities. Snags involve the patient abandoning courses of action on the assumption that others would oppose them or because they are assumed to be forbidden or dangerous. These sorts of dysfunctional beliefs are also challenged in COGNITIVE BEHAVIOUR THERAPY and RATIONAL EMOTIVE THERAPY. (Ryle, 1990)

COGNITIVE BEHAVIOUR THERAPY (CBT) is an adaptation of BEHAVIOUR THERAPY which accepts inner events (so does not focus narrowly on behaviour alone). After great popularity in psychiatry and clinical psychology in the 1960s, the limits of behaviour therapy's success, by only focusing on behaviour and ignoring the subjective view of the client became obvious. For this reason some behaviour therapists adapted the method and applied it to inner events (Cautela) and to an alliance with the client to take charge of their behaviour (the 'self-control theory' of Kanfer and Karoly). Sometimes CBT is simply called 'cognitive therapy', though confusingly the latter term also covers a range of approaches including COGNITIVE ANALYTICAL THERAPY, PERSONAL CONSTRUCT THERAPY and RATIONAL EMOTIVE THERAPY. The common concern of the cognitive therapies is to work with the interaction of thought, feelings and action. It is important to emphasise that CBT was driven by the pragmatics of clinical work, by psychiatrists like Aaron Beck. Its relationship with COGNITIVISM in academic psychology is questionable as these clinical innovations were developed *before* changes were apparent in academic psychology during the 1980s. So although cognitive therapists now often use the language of cognitivism in their writings, CBT is only tenuously connected to theories developed in academic psychology. CBT is increasingly the commonest form of therapy available to patients in the NHS, although PSYCHODYNAMIC THERAPY has a strong tradition, especially within medical psychotherapy (psychiatrists who practise as therapists rather than focus on drug treatments). (Cautela, 1973; Beck, 1976; Branch & Dryden 2008)

COGNITIVISM is a major branch of academic psychology emphasising internal mental processes, which became popular in the late twentieth century, displacing BEHAVIOURISM as the main expression of a scientific study of human action. Like BEHAVIOURISM it assumes that EMPIRICISM (building up knowledge via the senses) remains the basis of objective psychological knowledge. It assumes further that inner events and representations (perceptions, thoughts, language, images, judgements and memories) can be studied systematically and experimentally and predictable patterns identified from these empirical methods. It has been criticised by HUMANISTS and POSTMODERNISTS for this assumption. These critics emphasise the importance of context-specific meanings, which are not amenable to scientific generalisations. (Eysenck & Keane, 2000)

COUNTER-TRANSFERENCE (see TRANSFERENCE)

ECLECTICISM is a term used to describe the incorporation or integration of different theoretical assumptions when carrying out a task. It is justified usually on pragmatic grounds (trying different things to see what works). It is criticised sometimes for the inevitable incoherent connection between theory and practice. The next entry explains its association with therapy.

ECLECTIC or INTEGRATIVE THERAPIES include elements of several therapies. Examples are COGNITIVE ANALYTICAL THERAPY, NEURO-LINGUISTIC PROGRAMMING and SOLUTION-FOCUSED BRIEF THERAPY. As therapies are practical attempts to help people change, it is not surprising that over the years models appear which attempt to adopt the best parts of previous ones. As with the term 'HUMANISTIC THERAPY', 'eclectic' or 'integrative' could be applied fairly widely. Even what appear to be original or pure models, such as PSYCHOANALYSIS, GESTALT THERAPY and BEHAVIOUR THERAPY, are derived or have learned from philosophies from antiquity or the East. (Feltham & Horton, 2006; O'Brien & Houston, 2007, Worsley, 2007)

EMPIRICISM is a form of philosophy which builds up knowledge (both everyday and scientific) via the senses. Put simply, it is what scientists agree about what they hear, see, smell, taste or touch. Unlike PHENOMENOLOGY and EXISTENTIALISM, which emphasise unique experience, empiricism is about a stable or repeatable *consensus* about observations across a number of observers. These observations are then recorded as objective facts. The method is then extended to experimentation, where scientists test hypotheses. By holding all conditions constant and then introducing a new condition they observe the impact of the latter. In this way they test hypotheses and deduce knowledge from experimentation. Thus empiricism includes systematic observation and experimentalism.

EXISTENTIALISM is a form of philosophy that focuses on the close experiential study of human existence – what it means to be human. Its ancient roots can be found in Buddhism and its modern expressions can be found in forms of both Christianity (e.g. Kierkegaard) and atheism (e.g. Sartre). Existentialists emphasise that we are self-conscious and thoughtful beings, who are constantly faced with choices about how to live our finite lives. With this common condition comes anxiety and guilt – the products of the struggle to confront or evade the authentic nature of our limited existence. Existentialism emphasises the contingent or context-specific aspect of being alive – this particular person in this particular time and place seeing their lives in a unique manner. These emphases suggest that there are huge limits to fixed methods in the scientific study of human beings. BEHAVIOURISM is rejected by existentialists (because of its antipathy to subjectivism – how we think about things, coming from our emotions and prejudices, for example). So too are any attempts by other forms of psychology (such as PSYCHOANALYSIS) to find predictable patterns in human conduct determined by forces outside of our contingent experience of choice, responsibility and unique reflection. Thus all existentialists are subjectivists but not all subjectivists are existentialists: only existentialists emphasise unique experience and the features of choice and responsibility.

EXISTENTIAL THERAPY is a form of therapy guided by the philosophy of EXISTENTIALISM. (Spinelli, 2007, Cooper XXXX)

FEMINIST THERAPY refers to types of therapy explicitly informed by feminism. Although this can apply to any therapeutic style, in practice the PSYCHODYNAMIC approach dominates. For example, the long-established Women's Therapy Centre in London is explicit about its psychodynamic style of service. Other influences though came from the humanistic consciousness-raising of the women's movement in the 1970s. Feminist therapy endeavours to avoid psychological reductionism (the process of explaining or interpreting all social activity by the characteristics of individuals) by retaining a commitment to the notion that the 'personal is political'. Without that commitment, feminist therapy would be defined very simply as a psychological treatment service for women by women. (Enns, 2004; Morris, 2005)

FUNCTIONAL MENTAL DISORDERS refer to psychiatric diagnoses which are based purely on the patient's speech and action and have no clear biological marker (such as evidence of neurological injury or disease, or evidence of biochemical changes demonstrated in a blood test). They constitute the great majority of psychiatric diagnoses (for example of 'anxiety states', 'depression', 'schizophrenia', 'bipolar disorder' and the 'personality disorders'). However, a neat division does not exist between these and 'organic mental disorders' with a proven or presumed physical cause, such as the dementias. Brain changes may only be identifiable post mortem and it is the way that the patient is speaking and behaving which tends to elicit the diagnosis – just as with the functional mental disorders. (Pilgrim, 2005)

GENERAL SYSTEMS THEORY (GST) was developed by the biologists Paul Weiss and Ludwig von Bertalanffy. They argued that human activity can only be properly understood as part of an open system. Open systems are constantly affected by their environment of context, whereas closed systems are isolated from these influences. For example, a physics laboratory experiment involves examining a closed system, whereas human scientists study people in their social context. Also systems involve activities of varying levels of organisation, with new characteristics emerging with each level. Cells, tissues, organs, organ systems, bodies, dyads, families, large groups, cultures, societies – entail more and more complex forms of organisation, with new qualities emerging at each level. One level is necessary for the other to exist but one level cannot be explained by another (the error of reductionism). The theory has been a central influence on the development of family therapy (especially under the early influence of Gregory Bateson, whose views also informed NEURO-LINGUISTIC PROGRAMMING). Also GST has been recruited by critics of the biomedical model in mental health work. It has reinforced the holistic biopsychosocial model in mental health work, which has resisted the tendency towards biological reductionism – the purely biomedical model – in psychiatry and psychological reductionism – the process of explaining or interpreting all social activity in individual terms – in psychology. (Pilgrim, 2002)

GESTALT THERAPY was created by the German physician Fritz Perls, who trained as a psychoanalyst. He abandoned the traditional psychoanalytical approach in favour of one addressing the patient's here-and-now experience. In particular, he emphasised the direct authentic encounter between the therapist and the patient. Perls incorporated ideas from Gestalt psychology (which studied the innate human capacity to identify whole patterns in their immediate perceived world), EXISTENTIALISM (Buber, Sartre and Tillich) and Eastern ways, especially Zen Buddhism. (Woldt & Toman, 2005)

HUMANISM is a philosophical position that puts humans rather than God or supernaturalism at the centre of its moral and social commitment. It is consequently associated with both secularism and rationalism. It prioritises mutual obligation between human beings and emphasises the role of reason and universal human rights. Inevitably, the great majority of humanists are atheists or agnostics, though there is some blurring with the liberal edge of organised religions, which also prioritises human relationships. Because Buddhism is not a deistic philosophy, but one focusing on direct experience and personal responsibility, it is readily embraced by humanists. The rejection of religious dogma extends often in humanism to political dogma. Its emphasis on liberalism, reason and an earthly concern for the common good makes it a ready platform for forms of psychological treatment. Its emphasis on human freedom and responsibility places it close to EXISTENTIALISM. The sixth-century Greek pantheists began this philosophical tradition and one of its founders, Thales, is credited with the maxim 'Know thyself'. Socrates is also a relevant philosophical prompt for today's HUMANISTIC THERAPY.

HUMANISTIC THERAPY is a broad description of treatment guided by the philosophy of HUMANISM. The term tends to be used especially to describe therapies that are phenomenological in approach (examining how the client sees their current world). However, it is a very loose term – an argument could be made that all forms of secular psychological therapy are humanistic in character. For example, the original humanistic concern of Socrates, who encouraged an exploratory dialogue to understand the person's life situation (the 'Socratic method'), is influential in both EXISTENTIAL PSYCHOTHERAPY and in COGNITIVE BEHAVIOUR THERAPY.

IATROGENIC DETERIORATION EFFECTS are the negative outcomes of being in therapy. Just as medicinal treatments can produce 'side effects', which, more accurately, are undesirable or adverse *effects*, psychological treatments can be harmful. The term 'iatrogenic' means doctor-produced. This entry is highlighted because talking treatments may be thought of as being inevitably benign and may be contrasted with the dangers of drug treatment. This is a false dichotomy, as both forms of treatment pose risks (as well as offer benefits) to clients. Therapist abuse is the main source of deterioration effects but neglect and incompetence can also play their part in particular instances. (Gonssiorek, 1995)

MORAL TREATMENT developed in a number of countries in the late eighteenth century. It was an asylum regime partly influenced by religious and partly medical ideas about humane treatment on the one hand and order and regimentation on the other. This combination was aimed at reducing the lunatic's ALIENATION to bring them back into the moral fold of wider humanity. By the second half of the nineteenth century, biomedical assumptions displaced this moral emphasis, as medical superintendents increasingly dominated the asylum system, replacing 'lay' administrators. However, the assumptions of moral treatment continued to resonate in the twentieth century, with the development of the therapeutic community movement.

MULTIMODAL THERAPY was developed by the South African behaviour therapist Arnold Lazarus during the 1970s. He argued that any form of therapy should attend to the complex biological, internal and interpersonal aspects of the patient, which he coded with the acronym BASIC ID. These seven dimensions of personal functioning are behaviour, affect (emotions), sensations, images, cognitions (thoughts), interpersonal relationships and drugs/biology. This approach inevitably encourages forms of ECLECTIC THERAPY and is close to the TRANSTHEORETICAL MODEL. Its emphasis on holistic assessment of the patient also suggests its affinity with GENERAL SYSTEMS THEORY, although its notion of the social is largely limited to the interpersonal realm. (Palmer, 2006)

NARRATIVE THERAPY developed as a version of family therapy in the 1980s and is based on the proposition that therapy is a place for stories to be told, co-constructed (with actual or imagined audiences), re-told and re-constructed (again with actual or imagined audiences). This emphasis on 'storying' has found sympathetic therapists in PSYCHOANALYSIS, SOLUTION-FOCUSED BRIEF THERAPY and POSTMODERN THERAPY. (McLeod, 1997; White & Epston, 1990)

NEURO-LINGUISTIC PROGRAMMING is a set of techniques derived from a range of therapeutic approaches (including hypnosis and GESTALT THERAPY) aimed at altering the patient's view of the world and their flexibility within it. The view of the world or inner 'map' is shared with the therapist, who offers direct suggestions about change. The latter involves 'modelling' new ways of thinking and acting. Modelling occurs by direct influence from the therapist and by the therapist drawing attention to aspects of the patient's map that are already working well in order to enlarge and reproduce them. (Bandler & Grinder, 1975)

NORMALISATION is a term used by professionals in two overlapping ways. The first refers to a broad set of social and political measures to ensure full citizenship for those with mental or physical disabilities. Examples here would be about ensuring access to ordinary opportunities available to non-disabled fellow citizens. The second connotation of the word is for behaviour to be described as part of a normal range or for it to be rendered intelligible in its context. An example of this would be of re-casting a person's label of depression as understandable misery in the wake of loss in their lives. The latter connotation also describes a form of RE-FRAMING.

PERSONAL CONSTRUCT THERAPY is derived from the work of the American psychologist George Kelly and his 'personal construct theory'. He proposed that we all act as though we are scientists, constantly testing hypotheses, and each of us has a unique personal construct system – a unique way of seeing and interpreting our inner and outer world. If a hypothesis is confirmed, the person will retain a view of the world about that point of thought and action. If it is not confirmed the person then will re-construe their world or experience distress. Thus personal constructs systems tend to stabilise but they are also open to change. The role of the therapist is to understand how the patient construes their world currently and works with them to test out new hypotheses for enabling personal change. The emphasis on unique constructions places the theory close to that of EXISTENTIALISM but its cognitive emphasis also means that it is viewed favourably by other forms of cognitive therapies like CBT and CAT. Indeed in the early development of the latter, Kelly's work was explicitly utilised. (Kelly, 1955; Fransella, 2006)

PERSON-CENTRED THERAPY, which used to be known mainly as 'client-centred' counselling or therapy, is derived from the work of the American psychologist Carl Rogers and represents the purest version of HUMANISTIC THERAPY. Rogers began studying child development and this is reflected in his form of therapy focusing on the conditions of psychological growth. Rogers emphasised that therapy is about providing a facilitative relationship, in which the patient's own inner potential for growth could be nurtured. He identified three main aspects of this facilitative relationship: genuineness; warmth; and empathy. For Rogers these were necessary and sufficient to enable a person to change for the better. This emphasis on the innate capacity for self-development is consistent with the pragmatism and individualism of North American culture in the twentieth century. (Sanders 2006; Mearns & Thorne, 2007; Rogers, 1955)

PHENOMENOLOGY is the study of how people subjectively perceive the world. Its subjective emphasis places it near to EXISTENTIALISM. Occasionally in the therapy literature we find the terms linked, as in an 'existential-phenomenological approach'. However, strictly phenomenology is a *method* of investigation derived from philosophy (Hegel and Husserl), whereas existentialism is a complete philosophy. Also, it can be distinguished from traditional scientific methods, which seek to identify essential aspects of the world – attempts at the objective description of reality. Phenomenology is interested instead in the way that reality *appears* to people, not reality in and of itself.

POSTMODERN THERAPY refers to forms of psychological treatment shaped by the assumptions of POSTMODERNISM.

POSTMODERNISM is a description of a movement in recent social science that has abandoned older 'grand narratives' such as PSYCHOANALYSIS or BEHAVIOURISM, which offered complete theories of human conduct. Instead postmodernism suggests that all knowledge claims about human experience and behaviour are context-bound (specific to the situation) and reflect the unique view of the participants. As a result, like EXISTENTIALISM it rejects attempts to build a stable and permanent body of psychological knowledge. Instead all knowledge claims are seen as unstable and contestable.

PSYCHOANALYSIS is a term used now to describe a range of approaches to understanding unconscious life following its founder, the Austrian physician Sigmund Freud. The idea of an inner cauldron of irrational life, which can be distinguished from external reality (defined by rational consensus), is traceable to the Ancient Greek philosopher Heraclitus. Thus Freud did not 'discover' the unconscious but he provided us with a modern rationale for its relevance in everyday life. Not only was his approach modified by his early followers (especially Carl Jung and Alfred Adler), Freud radically revised his theory in his own lifetime. After his death, three main strands of psychoanalysis were established. The first, continued by his daughter Anna Freud, now tends simply to be called 'Freudian psychoanalysis'. The second strand is based on the ideas of the lay (non-medical) analyst Melanie Klein and focused on the innate drive of aggression more than Freud. The third is an important group (independent of Freud and Klein) who developed the idea that the internalisation of early personal relationships (confusingly called 'object-relations') was central to understanding our personal lives as we grow. Both Klein and the 'Independents' are called 'object-relations' theorists. All three strands emphasise early life and all use interpretation as the main therapeutic intervention.

PSYCHODRAMA involves the use of dramatic reconstruction of personal problems in a group therapy setting. It was developed in Vienna and then New York by its founder Jacob Moreno, who transferred the methods of role play with children to adults. It is a form of directed group therapy in which group members take it in turns to work on their problems using their peers to play parts in current or past scenarios in their lives.

PSYCHODYNAMIC THERAPY (also to be found as 'dynamic' or 'psychoanalytical' psychotherapy) is a broad description of any form of psychological treatment that is derived from the work of Freud and his loyal or dissenting followers. Like PSYCHOANALYSIS, it emphasises the use of interpretation to understand the unconscious life of patients. In particular, interpretations are directed at understanding RESISTANCE, TRANSFERENCE, COUNTER-TRANSFERENCE and dreams. Successful therapy is based upon a good WORKING ALLIANCE with the patient. It differs from PSYCHOANALYSIS proper in a number of ways. First, it is generally less intense (in terms of session frequency) and lengthy. Second, its practitioners do not have to be trained psychoanalysts. Third, it has the explicit aim of producing mental health gain for the client. By contrast, PSYCHOANALYSIS has the main aim of understanding the unconscious. (Jacobs, 2004; Klein 2006)

PSYCHOSYNTHESIS was developed by the Italian psychiatrist Roberto Assagioli in the early twentieth century. It is a form of ECLECTIC THERAPY that takes many of the assumptions of PSYCHOANALYSIS but also includes an exploration of aspects of the patient's intuition, aspirations and spirituality.

RATIONAL EMOTIVE THERAPY (RET), which is now known as 'rational emotive behaviour therapy' is derived from the work of the clinical psychologist Albert Ellis. He abandoned psychodynamic therapy in favour of a therapeutic method that more directly challenges the patient's view of themselves and their actions in the world. Ellis was influenced by STOICISM in the development of his theory. (Ellis, 1994; Dryden & Neenan, 2004)

RE-FRAMING refers to the ability of human beings to understand the world in a new way at the suggestion of another person.

The latter does not have to be a therapist (though therapists have used it explicitly and labelled it as a helpful process). When it is used in therapy, it challenges the client to move away from their current way of looking at and understanding a problem to another way, which offers more opportunity for change. The idea of re-framing starts from a relativist view of the world – that there is not a single external reality we must agree with but a range of ways of encountering the world. This point was first raised by Epictetus, but has been utilised by many styles of modern therapy. (Watzlawick et al, 1974)

RESISTANCE is a term associated mainly with PSYCHOANALYSIS but has been used by therapists from most schools. It reflects the assumption on the part of therapists that patients come along seemingly wanting to change but they resist efforts to make this happen in order to preserve the psychological status quo. For this reason, it includes any identifiable process inside the patient or within their personal relationships that works against therapeutic progress.

SKILLED HELPER MODEL is a practical approach to problem solving, which focuses on three core questions that might be addressed in combination or separately. What does the client think is the problem? What do they want instead? How might they get what they want? Thus current and prospective scenarios are rehearsed and the agency of the client (a combination of intention and action to make things happen) is appealed to in order to invite personal change. Developed by the American psychologist Gerard Egan, it attends to the therapist's genuineness, warmth and empathy emphasised by PERSON-CENTRED THERAPY. Its present–future orientation also links it to SOLUTION-FOCUSED BRIEF THERAPY and its mixture of cognitive and behavioural elements places it close to COGNITIVE BEHAVIOUR THERAPY. (Egan, 2006)

SOLUTION-FOCUSED BRIEF THERAPY (SFBT) is a set of techniques derived to help individuals and families change by focusing on solutions not problems. These techniques include asking the 'miracle question' (the patient is asked to imagine that overnight a miracle has happened and all their problems have disappeared), and scaling exercises. The latter ask the patient about a range of aspects of their functioning on a scale of 0–10 where 0 is very poor and 10 is perfect – where would they put themselves now? They are then asked to imagine coming back and they have improved by a couple of points – 'what would be different?' SFBT differs from many other forms of therapy – it tries to ignore problems ('problem talk') in favour of talking up strengths and solutions. It is interested in present–future connections, not present–past connections for the patient: it is about imagined futures and strategies of achieving them. (O'Connell & Palmer, 2003)

STOICISM was a philosophical movement in Greek and Roman times. Its relevance for modern psychological treatment was the position it took about the relationship between feelings and reason. Reason is needed to clarify the truth of a situation facing a person but it can be constantly diverted by his or her emotional reaction. In the pursuit of truth the Stoics cultivated self-discipline about thought and fortitude in the face of the inevitable distressing challenges and calamities of life. The Stoical position is accepted as a useful guide by many forms of therapy.

STRUCTURAL FAMILY THERAPY reflects the application of GENERAL SYSTEMS THEORY (GST) to family therapy. The term 'structure' refers in GST to the relatively stable or repeated patterns in a system. Each family has its unique patterns. Structural family therapists develop ways to understand these unique patterns and adopt a flexible approach to disrupt those structures, which are dysfunctional for one or more family members. (Minuchin & Fishman, 1981)

TRANSACTIONAL ANALYSIS (TA) is a form of therapy developed by the Canadian psychiatrist Eric Berne. He was influenced by his analysts, Paul Federn and Erik Erikson. From the former he developed the idea of ego states (parent, adult and child) and an understanding of psychotic patients. From Erikson he developed the idea of a person's unique 'life script'. From Freud he took the idea of repeated dysfunctional patterns and called them 'games' – the start of his most popular text *Games People Play*. The emphasis on a unique life story demonstrates the resonances of EXISTENTIALISM and PHENOMENOLOGY in TA. (Stewart, 2007)

TRANSFERENCE and COUNTER-TRANSFERENCE refer to the unconscious reactions of the patient to their therapist (transference) and vice versa (counter-transference). They reflect the projections of each party onto one another from their respective childhood histories. Sometimes the terms are used loosely to describe any thought or feeling emerging from each party in therapy outside of the rational business of fee paying and the WORKING ALLIANCE. The terms are used in therapies derived from, or influenced by, PSYCHOANALYSIS.

TRANSTHEORETICAL MODEL of therapy refers to the eclectic approach developed by James Prochaska and Carlo DiClemente during the 1980s. Whereas other forms of ECLECTIC THERAPY integrate a range of approaches, their work started explicitly as a critique of the limitations of single-model therapies. These were seen as limited to a particular frame of reference and so were insulated, unhelpfully, from the potential advantages of others. Prochaska and DiClemente argued that the advantages of a range of therapies should be harnessed for client change, according to differing needs. They also argued that some clients require little or no intervention as they may construct strategies for change on their own. (Jackson, 2006)

WORKING ALLIANCE is a term used by many therapists to indicate the rational, collaborative aspect of the therapeutic relationship, including an emotional bond, and agreements about the goals and tasks of therapy. It is distinguished from the non-rational aspects of TRANSFERENCE, COUNTER-TRANSFERENCE and RESISTANCE. The notion also appears as the 'therapeutic alliance', 'therapeutic bond' or 'working relationship' in the professional therapy literature.

Further reading

Bandler, R & Grinder, J (1975) *The Structure of Magic: A book about language and therapy.* Palo Alto CA: Science and Behavior Books.

Beck, AT (1976) *Cognitive Therapy and the Emotional Disorders*. New York: Meridian.

Branch, R & Dryden, W (2008) *The Cognitive Behaviour Counselling Primer*. Ross-on-Wye: PCCS Books.

Cautela, LR (1973) Covert processes and behavioural modification. *Journal of Nervous and Mental Diseases 157*, 27–36.

Cheshire, K & Pilgrim, D (2004) *A Short Introduction to Clinical Psychology*. London: Sage.

Cooper, M (2003) *Existential Therapies*. London: Sage.

Dryden, W & Neenan, M (2004) *The Rational Emotive Behavioural Approach to Therapeutic Change*. London: Sage.

Egan, G (2006) *The Skilled Helper: A Problem Management and Opportunity Development Approach to Helping* London: Routledge

Ellis, A (1994) *Reason and Emotion in Psychotherapy: Revised and updated*. New York: Birch Lane Press.

Enns, CZ (2004) *Feminist Theories and Feminist Psychotherapies: Origins, themes and variations*. Norwood NJ: Ablex.

Eysenck, MW & Keane, MT (2000) *Cognitive Psychology: A student's handbook*. London: Psychology Press.

Feltham, C & Horton, I (eds) (2006) *The Sage Handbook of Counselling and Psychotherapy*. London: Sage.

Fransella, F (2006) Personal construct counselling and psychotherapy. In C Feltham & I Horton (eds) *The Sage Handbook of Counselling and Psychotherapy*. London: Sage.

Gonssiorek, JC (ed) (1995) *Breach of Trust: Sexual exploitation by health care professionals and clergy*. London: Sage.

Hearnshaw, LS (1987) *The Shaping of Modern Psychology: An historical introduction*. London: Routledge.

Jackson, P (2006) The transtheoretical model. In C Feltham & I Horton (eds) *The Sage Handbook of Counselling and Psychotherapy* London: Sage.

Jacobs, M (2004) *Psychodynamic Counselling in Action*. London: Sage.

Kelly, G (1955) *The Psychology of Personal Constructs*. New York: Norton.

King, T (2006) The attachment theory of John Bowlby. In C Feltham & I Horton (eds) *The Sage Handbook of Counselling and Psychotherapy* London: Sage.

Klein, M (2006) *The Psychodynamic Counselling Primer*. Ross-on-Wye: PCCS Books.

Leuder, I & Thomas, P (2000) *Voices of Reason, Voices of Insanity*. London: Bruner/Routledge.

Lovell, K (2006) Behavioural psychotherapy. In C Feltham & I Horton (eds) *The Sage Handbook of Counselling and Psychotherapy* London: Sage.

McLeod, J (1997) *Narrative and Psychotherapy*. London: Sage.

Marks, IM (1987) *Fear, Phobias and Rituals*. Oxford: Oxford University Press.

Mearns, D & Thorne, B (2007) *Person-Centred Counselling in Action*. London: Sage.

Minuchin, S & Fishman, HC (1981) *Family Therapy Techniques*. Cambridge MA: Harvard University Press.

Morris, B (2005) *Discovering Bits and Pieces of Me: Research exploring women's experience of psychoanalytical therapy*. London: Women's Therapy Centre.

Murphy, G (1964) *An Historical Introduction to Modern Psychology*. London: Routledge.

O'Brien, M & Houston, G (2007) *Integrative Therapy*. London: Sage.

O'Connell, B & Palmer, S (eds) (2003) *The Handbook of Solution-Focused Therapy*. London: Sage.

Palmer, S (2006) Multimodal therapy. In C Feltham & I Horton (eds) *The Sage Handbook of Counselling and Psychotherapy* London: Sage.

Pilgrim, D (2002) The biopsychosocial model in Anglo-American psychiatry: Past, present and future? *Journal of Mental Health* 11(6), 585–94.

Pilgrim, D (2005) *Key Concepts in Mental Health*. London: Sage.

Rogers, CR (1955) Persons or science? A philosophical question. *American Psychologist 10*, 267–78.

Ryle, A (1990) *Cognitive-Analytic Therapy: Active participation in change*. London: Wiley.

Sanders, P (2006) *The Person-Centred Counselling Primer*. Ross-on-Wye: PCCS Books.

Screech, MA (1985) Good madness in Christendom. In WF Bynum, R Porter & M Shepherd (eds) *The Anatomy of Madness: Essays in the history of psychiatry Vol I*. London: Tavistock.

Spinelli, E (2007) *Practising Existential Psychotherapy*. London: Sage.

Stewart, I (2007) *Transactional Analysis Counselling in Action*. London: Sage.

Watzlawick, P, Weakland, JH & Fisch, R (1974) *Change: Principles of problem formation and problem resolution*. New York: Norton.

White, M & Epston, D (1990) *Narrative Means to Therapeutic Ends*. New York: Norton.

Woldt, A & Toman, SM (2005) *Gestalt Therapy: History, theory and practice*. London: Sage.

Worsley, R (2007) *The Integrative Counselling Primer*. Ross-on-Wye: PCCS Books.

Appendix
Useful addresses

Alcoholics Anonymous, PO Box 1, 10 Toft Green, York, YO1 7ND (01904 644026)

Anxiety UK (formerly The National Phobics Society, Zion Community Resource Centre, 339 Stretford Road, Hulme, Manchester, M15 4ZY (www.anxietyuk.org.uk)

British Association for Counselling and Psychotherapy, BACP House, 15 St John's Business Park, Lutterworth, Leicester, LE17 4HB (www.bacp.co.uk)

British Psychological Society, St Andrews House, 48 Princess Rd East, Leicester, LE1 7DR (www.bps.org.uk)

Depression UK, Self Help Nottingham, Ormiston House, 32–36 Pelham Street, Nottingham, NG1 2EG (www.depressionuk.org.uk)

Gamblers Anonymous, PO Box 5382, London, W1A 6SA (020 7384 3040 www.gamanonymous.org.uk)

Institute of Family Therapy, 24–32 Stephenson Way, London, NW1 2HX (www.instituteoffamilytherapy.org.uk)

MDF The Bipolar Organisation, Castle Works, 21 St. George's Road, London, SE1 6ES (www.mdf.org.uk; www.mdfwales.org.uk)

Mental Health Foundation, London Office, 9th Floor, Sea Containers House, 20 Upper Ground, London, SE1 9QB (www.mhf.org.uk)

Mental Health Foundation, Scotland Office, Merchants House, 30 George Square, Glasgw, G2 1EG (www.mhf.org.uk)

MIND, Granta House, 15–19 Broadway, London, E15 4BQ (www.mind.org.uk)

Relate, Centreal Office, Premier House, Carolina Court, Lakeside, Doncaster, DN4 5RA (www.relate.org.uk)

Rethink, 89 Albert Embankment, London, SE1 7TP (www.rethink.org.uk)

Royal College of Psychiatrists, 17 Belgrave Square, London, SW1X 8PG (www.rcpsych.ac.uk)

Samaritans, The Upper Mill, Kingston Road, Ewell, Surrey, KT17 2AF (www.samaritans.org.uk)

Subject index

Name index

THE THERAPEUTIC RELATIONSHIP
PERSPECTIVES AND THEMES

SHEILA HAUGH & STEPHEN PAUL (EDS)

ISBN 978 1 906254 04 9

pp. 278, £20.00

The importance of the therapeutic relationship is explored within key modalities of psychotherapy: person-centred, psychodynamic, existential, gestalt, transactional analysis, cognitive behavioural therapy, relational and transpersonal approaches.

The place of power and oppression and the social context of the relationship in therapy are reviewed. The reader is invited to consider their own modality, their practice and their understanding of what really works in therapy.

As therapy moves from psychological tool to a greater focus on the nature and quality of the relationship itself, this book sums up and critically reflects on the different views of the therapeutic relationship. It offers new perspectives that empower the practitioner and illuminate theory, based in reflective practice. This is essential reading for therapists and teachers of therapy alike.

Simon Robinson, Professor of Applied and Professional Ethics, Leeds Metropolitan University

Sheila Haugh is a senior lecturer in psychotherapy at Leeds Metropolitan University.

Stephen Paul is director of the Centre for Psychological Therapies at Leeds Metropolitan University.

PCCS BOOKS
www.pccs-books.co.uk